Statistical Language Learning

Statistical Language Learning

Eugene Charniak

A Bradford Book

The MIT Press
Cambridge, Massachusetts
London, England

First MIT Press paperback edition, 1996

This book was set in Times Roman by TechBooks and was printed and bound in the United States of America.

Library of Congress Cataloging-in-Publication Data

Charniak, Eugene.
  Statistical language learning / Eugene Charniak.
    p. cm. — (Language, speech, and communication)
  Includes bibliographical references and index.
ISBN 0-262-03216-3 (HB), 0-262-53141-0 (PB)
  1. Computational linguistics   2. Linguistics—Statistical
methods.   3. Mathematical linguistics.   4. Artificial intelligence.
I. Title.   II. Series.
P98.5.S83C47   1993
410′.285—dc20

93-28080
CIP

To my parents in memoriam

Contents

List of Figures

Statistical Language Learning

Preface

This book aims to acquaint the reader with both the current state of the art in statistical language processing (with an emphasis on what this says about language learning) and the mathematical background necessary to understand the field. It grew out of my conversion from a more "traditional" artificial-intelligence natural-language-processing (AI-NLP) researcher to one primarily interested in statistical approaches to the subject, and it is aimed at people with a traditional computer science background. I believe there is a need for such a book. Let me briefly explain why.

I think it is fair to say that few, if any, consider the traditional study of language from an artificial-intelligence point of view a "hot" area of research. A great deal of work is still done on specific NLP problems, from grammatical issues to stylistic considerations, but for me at least it is increasingly hard to believe that it will shed light on broader problems, since it has steadfastly refused to do so in the past. Furthermore, there seems to be a very vulnerable underbelly to the entire enterprise. AI-NLP holds that people say and write things to accomplish certain ends—the most common one being to inform others of facts about the world. (Let us restrict ourselves henceforth to this reason. Getting this right is hard enough without worrying about lies, rhetoric, and the nature of fiction.) But one cannot communicate everything about the world at once. Thus communication by necessity assumes that the listener knows something about the world and the speaker or author is simply trying to augment this in certain ways. Furthermore, the speaker/author's use of this assumption affects the way information is delivered. For example, if asked what Alice is doing we might respond, "She went to the supermarket." One does not add that she is, say, shopping for groceries. It is assumed that the knowledge listeners bring to the conversation enables them to fill this in for themselves. Thus language comprehension from an AI point of view assumes that language understanding depends on a lot of "real-world knowledge" and that our programs must have it if they are ultimately to succeed. Fortunately, there is a branch of AI—knowledge representation—whose purpose in life is to provide this knowledge, or at least provide a formalism in which we can encode this knowledge without too much difficulty. Thus we in AI-NLP go about our business not worried unduly by the fact that we do not actually have the knowledge base required by our most basic assumptions.

There is nothing wrong with this model as far as it goes. But at the same time anyone familiar with AI must realize that the study of knowledge representation—at least as it applies to the "commonsense" knowledge required for reading typical texts such as newspapers—is not going anywhere fast. This subfield of AI has become notorious for the production of countless non-monotonic logics and almost as many logics of knowledge and belief, and none of the work shows any obvious application to actual knowledge-representation problems. Indeed, the only person who has had the courage actually to try to create large knowledge bases full of commonsense knowledge, Doug Lenat (for example, see [27]), is believed by everyone save himself to be failing in his attempt. I for one have routinely told graduate students to stay away from the area. Thus many of us in AI-NLP have found ourselves in the position of basing our research on the successful completion of others' research—a completion that is looking more and more problematic. It is therefore time to switch paradigms.

The statistical approach has several attractions to one looking for another way to attack NLP problems. First, because it is obviously grounded in real text, and because it aims (at least so far) at problems where lack of perfection can be overlooked (such as speech recognition), statistical techniques have promise of producing usable results. Second, they offer an obvious way to approach learning—one simply gathers statistics—and I have yet to meet the person completely immune to the attractions of this AI subdiscipline.

However, moving to the statistical approach is by no means easy. Much of the background material is not common in computer science curricula, and many of us (e.g., I myself up to two years ago) simply do not know it. Needless to say, when I went to teach statistical NLP to my students, they did not have the necessary background either. Hidden Markov models (HMMs) are a good example. They are a staple of the engineering approach to NLP, particularly in speech recognition, but are covered hardly at all within computer science.

If I am right in my negative assessment of traditional AI-NLP, there are going to be a lot more computer-science-trained people who want to move out of AI-NLP and, perhaps, into statistical NLP. These people too need to learn these new ropes. Thus I felt that a book on statistical approaches to NLP was needed, and particularly one aimed at people with a computer-science background. Making the further restriction to statistical learning of language was an easy decision. Learning has always been of central importance to AI, and the beauty of statistical approaches is the extent to which they make learning easy, or at least possible.

Mathematics is a convenient tool for expressing statistical ideas and is used throughout this book. Nevertheless, I have tried to make this book accessible to those without an extensive mathematical background. In particular:

• Chapter 2 gives a quick introduction to (review of) the basic probability theory needed in the rest of the text.

• The most mathematically complicated chapters, 4 and 6, can be postponed, or skipped altogether, if the reader is not interested in implementing (or fully understanding) the basic algorithms they describe.

• I have tried to make the mathematical derivations simple by keeping the steps between one equation and the next small. This, of course, has the paradoxical effect of making things look very scary indeed, if only through sheer bulk of notation.

There are thus several possible paths through this book and the reader should not feel constrained to follow the chapters in the order presented. The inter-chapter dependencies look like this:

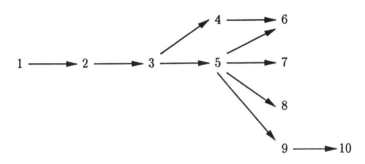

Chapters 1, 2, and 3 give introductory material, on (1) AI natural-language processing, (2) probability and information theory, and (3) hidden Markov models, upon which the rest of the chapters depend. Chapter 4 gives the mathematical underpinnings of many HMM algorithms. Chapter 5 introduces probabilistic context-free grammars. Chapter 6 gives their more mathematical underpinnings and requires chapter 4, but otherwise chapters 4 and 6 are not required for the rest of the book. Finally, chapters 7, 8, 9, and 10 cover probabilistic context-free grammar learning, syntactic disambiguation, semantic word classes, and lexical disambiguation, respectively. They can be read independently of one another except that chapter 10 uses many of the techniques in chapter 9.

Because the book is relatively self-contained, it could be used at the intermediate or advanced undergraduate level. However, because of its narrow focus, and because it skirts so close to the research edge in this area, it would probably be better as a beginning graduate-level course. I have taught both graduates and undergraduates using previous drafts.

Which brings me to the customary, but nevertheless heartfelt, thanks to my students who read and commented on earlier drafts: Curtis Hendrickson, Neil Jacobson, and Mike Perkowitz. Special thanks go to Felix Yen, whose comments were particularly useful.

1 The Standard Model

1.1 Two Technologies

Over the last 30 years or so there has developed within the artificial intelligence and computational linguistics communities a technology for allowing computers to understand language, at least to a limited degree. This technology has now reached the point that commercially useful products can be based on it. Unfortunately, such products can be used only in limited domains where complete accuracy is not required, as a program that can fully understand English (the only language we really deal with here) is still far beyond both our technology and our scientific understanding. One application being pursued is database classification of documents such as newspaper articles. A machine that could scan newspapers, pick out those dealing with, say, forest fires, and then enter the information into a database would be useful even if it missed some articles, accidentally included an occasional article off the topic, or sometimes got the details of the fire wrong. Even if higher accuracy is required, such a program could still be justified as a helper to a human database "stuffer."

Over approximately the same period, a second technology has been developing within the engineering and acoustical communities to help speech-recognition systems figure out what a speaker is saying. Quite often (practically always, in fact), systems designed to identify words using only the speech signal cannot uniquely determine the correct word. They might have a hard time distinguishing, say, "merry" from "very" or "pan" from "ban." Yet the context often overcomes this, as in "Please hand me the ???." or "The choice you made was ??? good." That is, we can think of the problem of speech recognition as having two parts: extracting the most likely words from the signal and deciding among these possibilities using the information from the surrounding words. The second of these requires knowledge about the language.

The technologies referred to in the last two paragraphs are quite different. The NLU (natural-language understanding) community has developed programs for tasks like parsing sentences, assigning semantic relations to the parts of a sentence, etc. On the other hand, the speech-recognition community has developed statistical techniques for predicting the next word on the basis of the words so far. Neither technology has been completely successful. The NLU technology is still too brittle for comfort and requires a lot of human retooling to move from one domain to another, while the absence of anything like "understanding" places distinct limits on the statistical technology's ability to choose the right word when the acoustical part of the speech recognizer confuses them.

For these reasons, the last five years or so have seen the development of a subcommunity that is trying to combine these technologies. This can be done in many ways. The work we concentrate on here uses statistical techniques to learn the kinds of processing that the NLU community has developed, e.g., using statistical techniques for learning a grammar. (An alternative is to take traditional NLU work and add statistical tests for some particularly difficult problems.) We have concentrated on statistical language learning in part because it lends coherence to what would otherwise be a bewildering set of techniques. But equally important, the idea of learning a language is a fascinating one in its own right, and it is interesting to see how far statistical methods take us and how they can be improved.

In the rest of this chapter we review the basic tools from NLU work that are also used in statistical approaches. We make no effort to try to represent the work in this area fairly. Rather, we have restricted ourselves to those NLU ideas and tools that crop up again in a statistical guise.

1.2   Morphology and Knowledge of Words

The analysis of written language is typically divided into four parts: morphology, syntax, semantics, and pragmatics. To a first approximation these deal with the structure of words, the structure of sentences, the meaning of individual sentences, and how sentences relate to each other, respectively. In this chapter, and indeed throughout this book, the major emphasis is on syntax, since that is where most of the statistical work has concentrated.

Often we refer to words as *lexical items*; a *lexicon* is a structure that keeps track of the words (and possibly information related to them). Morphology is the study of the structure of individual words. For example, the word "going" is normally viewed as the word "go" with the suffix "-ing" added to the end. Similarly, the word "cats" is viewed as "cat" + "s," where the "s" converts the *singular* noun "cat" to the *plural* noun "cats." The form without the suffix is called the *root form*. Most of the structure of English words comes from suffixes, but there are prefixes as well, as in "disloyal" or "uncooperative." In the case of verb and noun endings, it clearly pays to record only the root forms for most words and derive the other forms from appropriate rules. This requires a morphological analysis program that finds the roots of words.

Part of speech (symbol)	Example
noun (noun)	dog, equation, concerts
pronoun (pro)	I, you, it, they, them
possessive (pos)	my, your
verb (verb)	is, touch, went, remitted
adjective (adj)	red, large, remiss
determiner (det)	the, a, some
proper noun (prop)	Alice, Romulus
conjunction (conj)	and, but, since
preposition (prep)	in, to, into
auxiliary verb (aux)	be, have
modal verb (modal)	will, can, must, should
adverb (adv)	closely, quickly
wh-word (wh)	who, what, where
final punctuation (fpunc)	. ? !

Figure 1.1
Examples of English parts of speech

English words are normally assigned to one or more *part-of-speech* categories. A part of speech is a set of words that have similar syntactic properties. Many of these are familiar to all of us—nouns, verbs, adjectives, and adverbs come to mind. Examples of the parts of speech considered in this text are given in figure 1.1.

Most linguistic theories also assume that words have *features*. The most common feature is the one we mentioned in passing when discussing the structure of "cats," that is, the distinction between singular and plural nouns. This is called the number feature. The next most common feature is person. That is, "I" and "we" are first-person pronouns, while "you" is a second-person pronoun. Figure 1.2 illustrates number and person by giving pronouns that have each feature. The features of number and person apply also to English verbs because of the rule of *subject-verb agreement*, which states that the subject of a verb must agree with the verb in number and person: one says "The dogs eat" but "The dog eats." That is, the form of the verb

	Singular	Plural
1st person	I, me, mine	we, us, ours
2nd person	you, yours	you, yours
3rd person	she, him, its	they, them, theirs

Figure 1.2
Some pronouns according to number and person

"to eat" for third-person-plural subjects like "the dogs" is "eat," while that for third-person-singular subjects is "eats."

1.3 Syntax and Context-Free Grammars

After morphology, the next step in moving from a string of words to its meaning is assigning it a *syntactic structure*. Ultimately, we are interested in teasing out the meaning of a sentence because we expect it to be useful for other purposes. We are interested in syntactic structure because it helps in determining the meaning. Consider the sentence

In the hotel the fake property was sold to visitors.

Native speakers of English have no trouble understanding this sentence; indeed, it takes some effort to see how much we bring to this process. For example, how do we know that:

• "in the hotel" does not modify "property" but rather "sold"?
• "the fake" modifies "property" and not, say, "hotel"?
• the "visitors" were buying property, not selling it?
• if the sentence had said "sold *by* visitors," they would have been selling the property?

We know this because of our knowledge of English grammar. In the mechanisms developed here, this knowledge is expressed by creating syntactic structures such as that in figure 1.3.

One builds such structures with a *grammar*, a specification of the permitted structures in a language. The most common kinds of grammar are the *context-free grammars* (CFGs), which consist of:

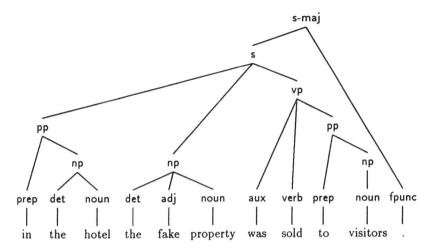

Figure 1.3
A syntactic structure

• a set of *terminal symbols*, the symbols that appear in the final strings (in our case the words and punctuation of English)

• a set of *non-terminal symbols*, symbols that are expanded into other symbols (in figure 1.3 these are the parts of speech plus np, vp, s, and s-maj)

• a specific non-terminal designated as the starting symbol (s-maj in our example)

• a set of *rewrite rules* each of which has a single non-terminal on the left-hand side and one or more terminal or non-terminal symbols on the right

(To be completely general we would also have to allow the rule whereby the starting symbol can go to the empty string, but this is not of interest to us.) The non-terminals we use include:

Non-terminal (symbol)	Examples
major sentence (s-maj)	"Jack ate." , "Who hit the dog?"
sentence (s)	"Jack ate" , "Who hit the dog"
verb phrase (vp)	"ate", "hit the dog"
noun phrase (np)	"Jack", "the dog", "it"
prepositional phrase (pp)	"to the zoo", "from me"

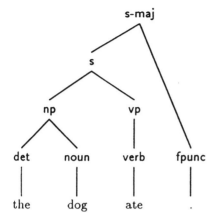

Figure 1.4
A simple syntactic structure

s-maj	→	s fpunc	det	→	the
s	→	np vp	noun	→	dog
vp	→	verb	verb	→	ate
np	→	det noun	fpunc	→	.

Rules—part (a)

vp	→	verb np	noun	→	salespeople
vp	→	verb np np	verb	→	sold
np	→	det noun noun	noun	→	biscuits
np	→	noun			

Rules—part (b)

Figure 1.5
Some context-free rules

For the example in figure 1.4 we would need the rewrite rules of figure 1.5(a).

A context-free grammar thus assigns one or more structures to every sentence in the language it defines. If any sentence is assigned more than one structure, the grammar is said to be *ambiguous*. English is, of course, ambiguous. For example, if our grammar includes the rules of figure 1.5(a) and (b), then the sentence "Salespeople sold the dog biscuits." would have the two parses indicated in figures 1.6 and 1.7. In the first of these it is dog

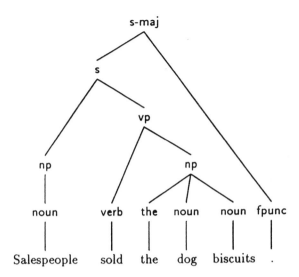

Figure 1.6
First structure for an ambiguous sentence

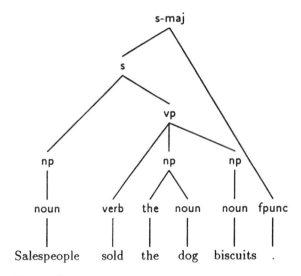

Figure 1.7
Second structure for an ambiguous sentence

biscuits that are being sold, while in the second it is simply biscuits that are being sold, and they are being sold to a dog.

It is possible to place restrictions on the form of context-free grammars without losing any real expressive power. One of the most common of such restrictions is *Chomsky-normal form*. A context-free grammar in Chomsky-normal form is like a regular context-free grammar, except all of the rewrite rules must be in one of two forms: *non-terminal → terminal*, or *non-terminal → non-terminal non-terminal*.

In other cases limits are put on the kinds of non-terminals that the grammar may contain. The most common of these is to require that all non-terminals be named using part-of-speech symbols with one or more bars above them, as in $\overline{\overline{\text{noun}}}$ (pronounced "noun-bar") or $\overline{\overline{\text{verb}}}$. By itself this is just a funny way to name non-terminals. But it can be made more than that by placing restrictions on the kinds of rules in which bar categories can be used. The standard restriction is that any non-terminal of the form $\bar{x}$ must expand into something containing an x. Second, there is typically a limit on how many bars can be used, for instance, no more than three bars on a non-terminal. This convention originated in a theory by Jackendoff called the $\overline{X}$ *theory* [15,29]. This was a detailed theory of English syntax and as such included many more restrictions and embellishments. However, the bar convention is now used more broadly, and that is how we are using it.

Before finishing our introduction to context-free grammars, we must note that it is not clear that the syntax of English can be fit into the context-free formalism; even if it can, parts of it are a tight fit at best. For example, consider the rule of subject-verb agreement mentioned above. A context-free grammar rule of the form "s → np vp" does not capture this regularity since it does nothing to prevent the np from expanding into a plural noun phrase (e.g., "the dogs") while the vp expands into a singular verb (e.g., "eats," giving "The dogs eats"). It is possible to fix this by *multiplying out features*. That is, to handle the regularity with regard to singular and plural, one would replace the non-terminals np and vp with four categories np-singular, np-plural, vp-singular and vp-plural, and then replace the single rule "s → np vp" with two rules "s → np-singular vp-singular" and "s → np-plural vp-plural." If one wanted to cover both number and person agreement one would need 12 categories (2 non-terminals · 2 number features · 3 person features); thus the term "multiplying out."

Another standard problem with context-free grammars is *long-distance dependencies*. In *wh-questions* (questions that start with a wh-word like "who"), the wh-word seems to "belong" to a place later in the sentence. For example, in "Whom did Fred give the ball to?" the "Whom" in some sense serves as the noun phrase in the prepositional phrase "to whom." This is called a "long-distance dependency" because a) it is a *dependency* (the prepositional phrase missing its noun phrase depends on the noun phrase earlier in the sentence) and b) it is *long-distance* in that the distance between the two parts of the dependency can be arbitrarily large, as in "Whom does Alice believe Fred wants to give the ball to?" This problem can also be solved within a context-free grammar, although it gets a bit complicated. The solution requires introducing *slash categories* [23]. These are new non-terminals like s/np (read "s slash np"), vp/np, etc. The intuitive meaning of s/np is that this category is like a normal s, but at some point lacks an np where there should be one. We then introduce a rule like "s → wh s/np" (this is not exactly correct, but it is good enough for our purposes), which indicates that when a wh-word starts the sentence the rest of the sentence is missing an np at some point. Of course, we then need rules like "s/np → vp," "s/np → np vp/np," "vp → verb np pp/np," etc.

We have emphasized the limitations of context-free grammars because it is important to realize that despite the emphasis we give them later, they do have their problems. Nevertheless, their prominence is understandable. Despite their simplicity, they allow the expression of a wide variety of English constructs while supporting efficient algorithms for many important language-comprehension tasks, most notably parsing, to which we turn next.

1.4 Chart Parsing

Given a context-free grammar and a sentence, we need to be able to find the structures for the sentence according to the grammar. An algorithm for doing this is called a *context-free parser*. There are many well-established techniques and covering all of them would be beyond the scope of this book. (See [43] for a good survey.) Instead, we discuss one particular parsing scheme, *chart parsing*, which is common in both NLU work and the statistical literature.

A chart parser has three main data structures, a *key list*, a *chart*, and a set of *edges*. A chart is a set of *chart entries* each of which consists of the name of a terminal or non-terminal symbol (e.g., a noun phrase or a preposition), the starting point of the entry, and the entry's length (e.g., the noun phrase

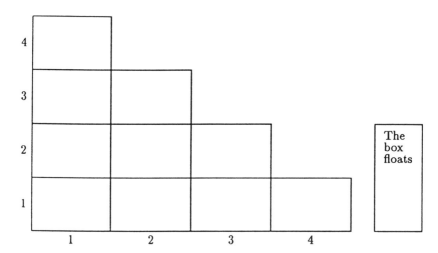

Figure 1.8
An empty chart at the start of a sentence

starts at location 2 and is three words long). Locations (for starting points) are the word numbers, starting with word 1. The chart entries are indexed by starting points and length.

The second data structure, the key list, is a pushdown stack of chart entries that are waiting to be entered into the chart. The only two things that can be done to the key list are adding things to and removing things from the front of the list.

The last of the three data structures, *edges*, indicate rules that can be applied to chart entries to build them up into larger entries. Figure 1.8 shows the empty chart and the key list at the start of the sentence "The box floats." The horizontal indicators for the chart (ranging in figure 1.8 from 1 to 4) indicate the starting position of a chart entry. The vertical indicators (from 1 to 4) indicate constituent length. So, for example, the bottom right square is where we write down constituents of length 1 starting at word 4, while the top left is where we indicate constituents of length 4 starting at word 1 (which would be constituents that covered the entire sentence). The algorithm for chart parsing is given in figure 1.9. In our example we use the grammar fragment of figure 1.10.

Edges keep track of the rules the algorithm is currently applying to the input. Each edge indicates: (1) the rule being tried, (2) the position where the first constituent of the right-hand side of the rule started (and thus where

To fill in the chart:

Loop while entries in key list

    1 Remove the entry from the key list.

    2 If entry is already in chart, go to next iteration of loop.

    3 Add entry from key list to chart.

    4 For all rules that begin with entry's type, add an edge
        for that rule to the chart.

    5 For all edges that need the entry next, add an extended edge.

    6 If the edge is finished, add an entry to the key list
        with appropriate type, start point, and length.

To extend an edge e with the chart entry c:

    1 Create a new edge e'.

    2 Set start(e') to start(e).

    3 Set end(e') to end(e).

    4 Set rule(e') to rule(e) with ∘ moved beyond c.

Figure 1.9
The algorithm for chart parsing

the finished constituent begins), (3) the position where the first uncompleted constituent on the right-hand side must start, and (4) the place on the right-hand side where the already found constituents end, and thus where the ones still needed will start. All the edges are drawn at the bottom of the chart; however, they interact with constituents at all levels of the chart.

As an example, we parse the sentence "The box floats." according to the algorithm in figure 1.9, using the grammar of figure 1.10. Consider the chart after the word "the" has been processed, as shown in figure 1.11. (In this and later charts we often omit chart sections that are empty.) The first key-list entry, "the," is removed according to step 1 of the algorithm. An identical entry is not in the chart already (we consider later how this could happen), so we add "the" to the chart in the position for an entry of length one starting at position one. Then an edge is added for all rules that could start with the constituent we just added. In the case at hand there is just one rule, "det → the," and it has been added as the edge at the bottom of the chart. Each edge indicates where the rule started (the tail of the arc) and where the next

s-maj	→	s fpunc	det	→	the
s	→	np vp	noun	→	box
vp	→	verb	verb	→	box
np	→	det noun	verb	→	floats
			fpunc	→	

Figure 1.10
Some context-free rules

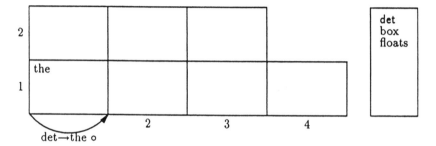

Figure 1.11
The chart after the first word

constituent must start (the head of the arc). It also gives the rule, and as part of the right-hand side of the rule it indicates by o how much of the rule has already been processed. Moving this indicator is part of "extending" edges, which is step 3 of the algorithm. More formally, extending an edge involves adding a new edge with (1) the same start point as the old one and its end at the end of the constituent we just added, and (2) moving the o to after the constituent in the right-hand side of the rule statement. In the case at hand, the constituent "the" is the last constituent, so the o goes at the end of the right-hand side. The presence of a o on the right-hand side of a rule also means that we have a new completed constituent here, so it is added to the key list, where, we can see, a det has been added to the top of this list. Note, by the way, that when extending an edge we *added* a new edge, but did not remove the old one. In general one should not remove an old edge, since an edge may be able to be extended in more than one way. (Consider the sentence "The girl drank the chocolate milkshake." and what happens to

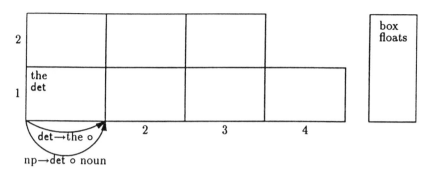

Figure 1.12
The chart after the determiner is entered

the rule "vp → verb np" after we first find the np "the chocolate" and later find the np "the chocolate milkshake.")

Returning to our example, we next process the det at the top of the key list. The result of this processing is shown in figure 1.12. The constituent was added to the chart and a new edge "np → det noun" is added because it starts with a det. Next "box" is taken from the top of the key list. This creates a noun entry, which is added to the chart next, extending the edge "np → det ○ noun." This finishes the edge, so a new constituent, np, is added to the key list. On the next loop through the algorithm the np is added to the chart, as is a new edge "s → np ○ vp." Some constituents and edges are added at this point that are in fact useless, but the parser creates them anyway. Since the word "box" can be a verb (as in "He will box ten rounds tomorrow"), a verb constituent is added to the chart at position (2,1), and since a verb can start a vp, an edge is added for this rule as well. (In fact, more sophisticated versions of chart parsing do not add these because there is no way a verb can be used at this point in the sentence, but we do not go into these schemes.) Figure 1.13 shows the chart after all of these constituents have been added (for the sake of readability, not all the edges are shown). By the end of the sentence the chart appears as in figure 1.14, where again we have omitted some edges.

Actually, chart parsing as just described does not produce syntactic structures like that in figure 1.6. It tells us if there is such a structure (just look for an s-maj at position (1,n) for an n-word sentence) and it lays out the position and lengths of other constituents, but it does not explicitly say how

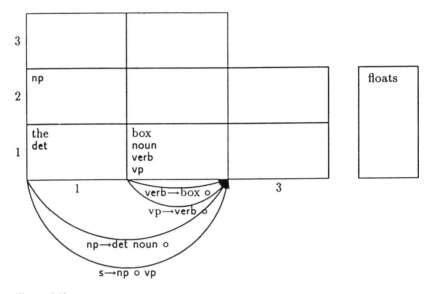

Figure 1.13
The chart just before working on "floats"

the legal structures are combined to build up one another. For example, while
it says that there is a s at position 1 of length 3, it does not say how that s
is built up. To have this information available, we would have to augment
our algorithm so that every constituent indicated which edges were used to
create it, and each edge indicated which chart entries were used to satisfy its
right-hand side. Later on we will need notation to talk about the non-terminal
N^j that spans the input words from the kth word to the lth word. We use the
expression $N^j_{k,l}$. Here we simply note that we associate with each such non-
terminal the set of completed edges that can create it, denoted as $\mathcal{E}^j_{k,l}$. The
set of completed edges that use $N^j_{k,l}$ on their right-hand side is denoted $\bar{\mathcal{E}}^j_{k,l}$.
We say the *set* of edges because a chart entry could be built up by several
different edges. For example, consider the chart for the parse of "Salespeople sold the dog biscuits." according to the grammar of figure 1.5(a and b).
The syntactic ambiguity shown in figures 1.6 and 1.7 indicates that there are
two ways of building up a vp at position 2 of length 4 (i.e., "sold the dog
biscuits"). The vps are built up by two different edges, one based upon the
rule "vp → verb np np" and one upon the rule "vp → verb np." Since we
need to enter this vp into the chart only once, the algorithm checks in step 2

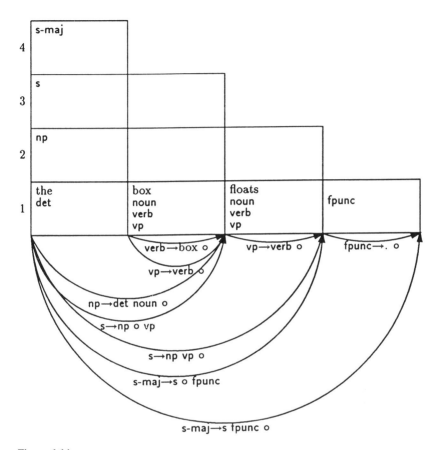

Figure 1.14
The chart at the end of the sentence

to see if the chart entry is already there. Figure 1.15 gives a version of the chart-parsing algorithm that keeps track of the edge information needed to construct the parse trees, with the additions in italics.

Once we have added the information about how constituents are built up, we can thread our way down all of the possible trees, starting with how the topmost s-maj could be built, down to the words. This would be efficient in the sense that producing a single parse tree would be quick and easy.

However, there is a complication here. If a grammar could have the two rules "a → b" and "b → a," a sentence could have an unbounded number of parse trees that could grow to an unbounded size. We thus insist that all grammars have no cycles like this. But even with this restriction, producing all possible parses could take a long time because the number of possible parses for an English sentence can, in general, grow exponentially.

Chart parsing does not, however, take exponential time. This is because, even with the further annotation of how constituents are built up, the chart in effect "summarizes" the possible parses without listing them explicitly. Indeed, given a grammar it is not too hard to convince yourself that the amount of work to produce a chart grows in the worst case as the cube of the length of the sentence. (The chart entries grow as the square, and each time we add a chart entry we need to look at all possible edges it might fit into, the number of which grows linearly in the length of the sentence.) But the number of parses can (and for real English, typically will) grow much faster. For example, consider what happens when a lot of prepositional phrases are crowded together at the end of a sentence, as in: "The president spoke to the nation about the problem of drug use in the schools from one coast to the other." Simply on the basis of syntax, the last pp ("to the other") could attach to any of the previous noun phrases (e.g, "the problem") or to the head verb, giving it six places to attach. The previous pp "from one coast" would have five places to attach, etc. If all of these attachment decisions were independent (they are not quite), then the total number of parses would be $6 \cdot 5 \cdot 4 \cdot 3 \cdot 2 \cdot 1 = 720$. The chart, on the other hand, needs to record only $6 + 5 + 4 + 3 + 2 + 1 = 26$ possible attachment possibilities. And while we made up this particular example, it is common to find English sentences being assigned thousands of parses. Thus any algorithm that requires enumerating all possible parses is generally considered too inefficient to be practical, a point that assumes some importance in chapter 6.

1.5 Meaning and Semantic Processing

Although you could not prove it by what we have said so far, it should come as no surprise that words, sentences, etc. have *meanings*. Indeed, some of them have more than one. For example, the word "bank" has one denoting a place to keep money and one denoting the side of a river. The meanings of a word are called its *senses*. Clearly "bank" has at least two senses and "to call" has even more (to telephone, to meet a bet, to yell to someone, to lead a square dance, to cancel a sports event). One part of understanding a text is to decide on the intended sense for a particular instance.

To fill in the chart:
Loop while entries in key list

    1 Remove the entry from the key list.

    2 If the entry is already in chart, *add the edge list of the entry to the edge list of the item already in in the chart and* go to next iteration of loop.

    3 Add entry from key list to chart.

    4 For all rules that begin with entry's type, add an edge for that rule to the chart.

    5 For all edges that need the entry next, add an extended edge.

    6 If the edge is finished, add an entry to the key list with appropriate type, start point, length *and edge list.*

To extend an edge e with the chart entry c:

    1 Create a new edge e'.

    2 Set start(e') to start(e).

    3 Set end(e') to end(e).

    4 Set rule(e') to rule(e) with ∘ moved beyond c.

    5 *Set the right-hand-side(e') to the right-hand-side(e) + c.*

Figure 1.15
Chart parsing while keeping track of completed edges

Now, before we can say much more about meanings we need some way to write them down. We do this by writing expressions in a formal language. In fact, we use the notation of the first-order predicate calculus, but we ignore quantifiers, variables, and most of what makes this language special. For example, the meaning of a noun phrase like "a yellow ball" would be

(and (spherical-ball ball-1)

    (color ball-1 yellow))

It is generally assumed that sentences (and by extension other phrases) get their meanings by combining the meanings of the individual words. This theory, called *compositional semantics*, is the only real account of people's ability to understand a virtually unlimited number of new and different sentences. To see how this might work, let us again consider the example "a yellow ball," this time concentrating on how the corresponding formal expression could be built up from parts. Here "yellow" contributes (color ball-1 yellow), which is intended to mean that the color of some specific ball, ball-1, is yellow. While this may seem to leave the nature of "yellowness" up in the air, it does, at least, distinguish this meaning of "yellow" from the one that means "lacking courage." In a similar way, "ball" contributes (spherical-ball ball-1), which is intended to mean that it is of type spherical-ball (as opposed to, say, social-ball).

Of course, we have not said how a program would decide that "yellow" refers to the color and "ball" refers to the toy. One useful if limited idea is *selectional restrictions*. The idea here is that particular senses place limits on how they can combine with other senses. For example, we might say that the sense not-courageous requires that the thing it modifies be human, or at least animate. Since neither possible meaning for "ball" is animate, this meaning of "yellow" is ruled out. Similarly, if we required the color yellow to modify a physical object (as opposed to a social event), then the other decision would be made.

Putting entire sentences together is more complicated. Typically we view this process as being organized around the main verb. For example, consider the sentence, "Alice gave the dog a bone." where "Alice" is assumed to denote Alice-1, "the dog" is assumed to denote the dog dog-2 and "a bone" denotes bone-3. If we assume that "give" denotes a three-place predicate in which the three places indicate the "giver," "recipient," and "given" respectively, then the meaning of the sentence would be something like:

(give Alice-1 dog-2 bone-3)

Note that there are different ways of saying the same thing, like: "Alice gave a bone to the dog.", "The dog was given a bone by Alice.", etc. The general idea is that all of these should map into the same formal language expression, or at least do so as much as possible, so that similarity of meaning is accompanied by similarity of formal expression. The rules that specify how pieces of the syntactic structure map into arguments of the formal language predicate are associated with the syntactic rules that build up the corresponding syntactic structure.

There is a lot more that could be said here. The actual form of the rules for going between syntactic form and the meaning representation turns out to be quite complicated when one gets down to all the details that would be required by a complete system. Nor have we discussed the problem of reference. Entities in a story or a conversation can often *co-refer*. We say two phrases co-refer when they refer to the same object. For example, in "Jack brushed his teeth with three tooth brushes and then threw them away." presumably "them" and "three tooth brushes" co-refer. From this example it should be clear that getting co-reference wrong can change the meaning of a sentence drastically. However, little of this kind of work has yet had much influence on the statistical study of language, if only because the latter, in trying to learn directly from the texts without creating a complicated theoretical superstructure, has not been able to tackle these issues. Thus we ignore them here, and introduce the little we need only in later chapters.

1.6 Exercises

1.1 Construct a chart for the sentence "The biscuits ate dog salespeople." according to the grammar of figure 1.5. Include all chart entries, whether or not they got into a complete parse. Indicate the more important edges that went into the complete parse.

1.2 Our chart-parsing algorithm can add constituents that have no hope of ever being incorporated into a complete parse, as for example in figure 1.14. (1) Which constituents there have this property? (2) Does any edge use these constituents to build up something that begins earlier in the sentence? (3) Suppose we restricted constituents to those for which the answer to (2) was "yes," i.e., those that an extant edge could use. Explain why this would fail at the beginning of a sentence. (4) Suppose any time a constituent of type x can occur next we add to the chart zero-length edges of the form $x \rightarrow \circ \ldots$ for each rule $x \rightarrow \ldots$. Explain how this solves the problem in (3). (5) Use these suggestions to reformulate the chart-parsing algorithm of figure 1.9 so that it never adds a chart entry that definitely cannot be fitted into a complete parse on the basis of what has already appeared in the sentence.

1.3 We stated that the attachment decisions for prepositional phrases at the end of sentences are not independent of each other. Explain why this is so. Hint: consider "I saw the statue with a telescope in the park." Under what circumstances can "in the park" modify "statue"? Diagram the relevant situations and suggest a general rule.

1.4 In addition to prepositional-phrase attachment, noun-noun attachment and adjective-noun attachment can create ambiguities. Show the ambiguity using the following phrases: bird feeder kit, song bird feeder kit, metal bird feeder kit, inexpensive bird feeder kit. Show that the same constraint suggested in the last exercise for prepositional phrases applies here as well.

1.5 It is possible for a CFG to have non-terminal symbols that cannot be expanded into strings of terminals. Give an example. Devise an algorithm that detects such cases.

1.6 Write a program that, given a CFG, outputs a corpus of approximately some desired size. (This is useful for creating corpora with known properties.) In cases where more than one rule can be used to expand a non-terminal, pick among the rules using a random number generator. Assume initially that all rules have equal likelihood of being chosen.

1.7 Anticipating the probabilistic CFGs (PCFGs) of chapter 5, modify the program of exercise 1.6 so that all rules have an associated probability (and the probabilities of the rules of each non-terminal sum to one). You might include a program that checks PCFGs for consistency. In particular, (1) implement the algorithm of exercise 1.5, which checks that all non-terminals can be expanded to terminal symbols, and (2) check each non-terminal to insure that the probabilities of its rules sum to one.

1.8 Write a chart parser. Be careful to implement your data structures cleanly, since we will extend this algorithm in chapter 6 to handle probabilistic CFGs.

2 Statistical Models and the Entropy of English

As stated in chapter 1, statistical language learning is based upon two technologies. The first, from artificial intelligence/computational linguistics, was covered in chapter 1. In this chapter we look at some of the probabilistic and information-theoretic foundations. In particular, the next section gives a quick review of the fragment of probability theory assumed in this book. Those familiar with probability theory can safely skip to the following section.

2.1 A Fragment of Probability Theory

Let X be the uncertain outcome of some event. We assume that this event has a finite number of possible outcomes (as opposed, for example, to an outcome that is a real number), and denote them by $V(X)$. X is called a *random variable*. (Actually, random variables are more general than this, but this extra generality need not concern us.) For example, if you are a doctor, X might be the disease your next patient has; in this case $V(X)$ ranges over all possible diseases. Or again, suppose you pick up a book (in English), open to some page and point at a word, all with your eyes closed. X would be the word you pointed to and would vary over the possible words of English. (We assume there is a fixed number of such words.) The probability of any particular outcome of an event is the fraction of the trials that this outcome is, in fact, the result. Formally, if x is a possible outcome of X (i.e., $x \in V(X)$) we denote the probability as:

$$P(X = x) \tag{2.1}$$

Often when there is no ambiguity about the event in question, we abbreviate this as $P(x)$. Returning to the example of picking a word at random, suppose you went through all your books and counted how many times each word of English occurred. Let W be the outcome of this event, and let w^i be the ith word of English. We assume there are ω different words. Let $|w^i|$ be the number of times the ith word appears in all the books. More generally, $|X = x|$ is the number of times the outcome of X is x. Then intuitively the probability of picking the ith word is:

$$P(W = w^i) \overset{\text{def}}{=} \frac{|w^i|}{\sum_{j=1}^{\omega} |w^j|} \tag{2.2}$$

We write this as a definition because it serves as our formal definition of an informal concept. And while we introduced the definition using the thought experiment of picking a word, nothing in it depends on that experiment, except the assumption that there is only a finite number of different words and the implicit assumption that there is only a finite number of books, so that all of the above numbers are finite.

It can be convenient to use the term $|\ U\ |$ for the denominator in equation 2.2, where U can be though of as the universe of all outcomes.

Often we have further information about the event. Suppose, for example, that we pick two words from our randomly selected book and that the two words are in a row. We can think of this as two different events, say W_1 and W_2. Now suppose you are told what the first word is and want to guess the second word. Obviously knowledge of the first word changes things. For example, before you knew anything, guessing "the" as the outcome would be a good bet (it is the most common word in English). But if you are told the first word is "the," then the second word is unlikely to be "the" as well. If you want to make a good guess, one thing to do is to look at every place in the books where "the" appears and collect statistics on the next word. More formally, you would find the *conditional probability*. The conditional probability of the outcome of an event based upon the outcome of a second event is defined as:

$$P(W_2 = w^j \mid W_1 = w^i) \stackrel{\text{def}}{=} \frac{\mid W_1 = w^i, W_2 = w^j \mid}{\mid W_1 = w^i \mid} \tag{2.3}$$

That is, to find out the probability that the second word is, say, "dog" given that the first word is "the," we find out the fraction of times that "the" is followed by "dog."

With these two definitions we can establish many of the most important relations between probabilities that are used here. Perhaps the most famous of these is *Bayes' law*:

$$P(x \mid y) = \frac{P(x)P(y \mid x)}{P(y)} \tag{2.4}$$

It is easy to show that this is true using the above definitions:

$$\frac{\mid x, y \mid}{\mid y \mid} = \frac{\mid x \mid / \mid U \mid \mid y, x \mid / \mid x \mid}{\mid y \mid / \mid U \mid}$$

This relation is useful when, as often, we are interested in finding the probability of some conclusion c given some evidence e because we want to pick the best (i.e., the most probable) conclusion. If we knew values of $P(c \mid e)$ for all of the conclusions then, we would be done. Typically we do not know these numbers. More often we know $P(c)$ and $P(e \mid c)$. For example, doctors are quite good at estimating the relative probability of a disease and how often a symptom is associated with a disease. (At any rate, they are better at this than at estimating $P(c \mid e)$.) This still leaves the denominator to calculate, but often we need not bother. Note that once we have fixed on the evidence the denominator stays the same for all of the conclusions. If we are simply interested in determining the most likely conclusion, then we can just set the denominator to, say, 1, and concern ourselves with maximizing the numerator. Alternatively, if we are concerned with getting the actual probabilities out and thus do need the correct denominator, we can use the following equality:

$$P(X = x) = \sum_{y \in V(Y)} P(X = x \mid Y = y)P(Y = y) \tag{2.5}$$

That is, to find out the probability of something happening, calculate the probability that it happens given some second event times the probability of the second event, and then sum over all possible outcomes of the second event. This can then be used to determine $P(y)$ in Bayes' law. A related equality that is often useful is

$$P(X = x) = \sum_{y \in V(Y)} P(X = x, Y = y) \tag{2.6}$$

This should be equally intuitive.

These relations, like all the others we will be looking at, generalize to the outcomes of several events. We can think of this in two ways. First, since we were not too specific in what we considered a single event, we could imagine that x and y above were each the outcome of a two-word-picking event. So perhaps $y =$ "the dog" while $x =$ "ate cauliflower." Alternatively, we can think of each word choice as a separate event and ask about something like $P(w, x \mid y, z)$. Substitution in equation 2.4 shows that Bayes' law generalizes in the obvious way:

$$P(w, x \mid y, z) = \frac{P(w, x)P(y, z \mid w, x)}{P(y, z)} \tag{2.7}$$

Another useful relation is:

$$P(w_1, w_2, w_3, \ldots, w_n) = P(w_1)P(w_2 \mid w_1)P(w_3 \mid w_1, w_2) \ldots$$
$$P(w_n \mid w_1, \ldots, w_{n-1}) \tag{2.8}$$

Substitution of the definitions shows this to be true. This relation also holds when the left-hand side is conditioned on some event, as in:

$$P(w_1, w_2, w_3, \ldots, w_n \mid x) = P(w_1 \mid x)P(w_2 \mid w_1, x)P(w_3 \mid w_1, w_2, x) \ldots$$
$$P(w_n \mid w_1, \ldots, w_{n-1}, x)$$

As before, substitution of definitions shows these to be true.

2.2 Statistical Models

Now let us turn to our topic. In its purest form, a statistical approach to learning English would take a body of English text (called a *corpus*) and learn the language by noting statistical regularities in that corpus. But few, if any, believe that this is possible. There are all too many regularities to be found and most of them are irrelevant, if not completely misleading. Thus we must add some knowledge of English (and perhaps some knowledge of the world) to our statistical brew in the hope that it enables our programs to find the *right* statistical regularities. However, our procedure is to look for the regularities and add knowledge only when simpler approaches fail.

We said at the outset that we wanted to learn the kinds of knowledge used in traditional NLU research. Nevertheless, our goal in this book is to learn a statistical (or probabilistic) model of English. Such a model has only one requirement, but it is one that many find uncongenial—it must assign a probability to all possible sequences of words. That is, for sequences of words of length n for some fixed n, we want to be able to assign a number to

$$P(W_{1,n} = w_{1,n}) \tag{2.9}$$

for all possible sequences $w_{1,n}$. Here $W_{1,n}$ is a sequence of n random variables $W_1, W_2 \ldots W_n$, each of which can take as its value any word of English (we assume there is a fixed number of them), and $w_{1,n}$ is a particular sequence of English words obtained by assigning each of the random variables a value.

One common objection to requiring a statistical model is that people cannot assign probabilities to sentences, so why should our machines? But it is not so clear that people cannot assign probabilities to word sequences, at least in a crude way. First, as shown in equation 2.8, we can break up the desired quantity (equation 2.9) into smaller components as follows:

$$P(w_{1,n}) = P(w_1)P(w_2 \mid w_1)P(w_3 \mid w_{1,2}) \ldots P(w_n \mid w_{1,n-1}) \tag{2.10}$$

Here we have adopted the standard abbreviation $P(w_{1,n})$ for $P(W_{1,n} = w_{1,n})$. Thus the problem of assigning probabilities to sequences can be reduced to the psychologically easier task of assigning probabilities to just the next word of a text. Consider the sentence "Jack went to the . . ." and the possible next words "hospital," "pink," "number," and "if" (the next word need not be the final one of the sentence). Most of us probably have reasonably accurate ideas about relative likelihoods of these words coming next, and turning these estimates into crude probabilities would not be hard. Indeed, experiments indicate that taking people's intuitions and turning them into probabilities is more accurate than any of the statistical methods currently available.

Often people find equation 2.10 confusing as it suggests to them that the probability of a word somehow depends only on the words before it and not those after it. This is a misinterpretation. In fact, this equation simply says that we can break up the probability of the *entire* sequence of words in a particular way. Note that we could break it up in another way, say starting with the last word and including a term for the probability of a word given those *after* it. Perhaps more to the point, nothing in equation 2.10 prevents a decision on a word from being influenced by the words coming after it. Consider a speech-recognition system that must decide between the words "big" and "pig" in the phrase

$$\text{The} \left\{ \begin{array}{c} \text{big} \\ \text{pig} \end{array} \right\} \text{dog} \dots$$

Suppose for the sake of argument that $P(\text{big} \mid \text{the}) = P(\text{pig} \mid \text{the})$, so that on the basis of only the first two words it is not possible to choose between "big" and "pig." However, consider the probability when we include word three:

$P(\text{the big dog}) = P(\text{the})P(\text{big} \mid \text{the})P(\text{dog} \mid \text{the big})$

$P(\text{the pig dog}) = P(\text{the})P(\text{pig} \mid \text{the})P(\text{dog} \mid \text{the pig})$

Since $P(\text{dog} \mid \text{the big})$ is much larger than $P(\text{dog} \mid \text{the pig})$, the sequence of words with the highest probability is "the big dog." Thus, in effect, the word "dog" selects "big" over "pig."

Another objection to statistical language models seems to arise from the assumption that such models are, by definition, crude word-counting affairs, like counting how many times the word "independence" appears in a text or how many times the word "watermelon" is followed by the word "seeds."

But one must distinguish between statistical *models* and statistical *methods*. The former do not require the latter. Indeed, a statistical model consisting of a person using intuition to make crude probability judgments is an example of a statistical model that does not use statistical methods.

We are saying, in effect, that prejudices against statistical models are really prejudices against *unsophisticated* statistical methods. Furthermore, there are reasons for wanting a good probabilistic model if we can get one: certain applications require it (e.g., speech recognition), and there is a good numeric figure of merit that can be used to compare such models (which we introduce in section 2.7).

2.3 Speech Recognition

Much of the statistical work on natural language was inspired by speech recognition. From a probabilistic point of view, the problem of speech recognition is to find the sequence of words $w_{1,n}$ that maximizes

$$P(W_{1,n} = w_{1,n} \mid \text{speech signal})$$

As we said in chapter 1, we want to divide this problem in two parts, one dealing with the acoustical aspects of speech and one just with language. We can do this formally by applying Bayes' rule:

$$P(w_{1,n} \mid \text{speech signal}) = \frac{P(w_{1,n})P(\text{speech signal} \mid w_{1,n})}{P(\text{speech signal})} \tag{2.11}$$

This is the quantity to be maximized, and since the denominator is the same for all $w_{1,n}$ we need only maximize the numerator. We note that the second term in the numerator expresses how well the speech signal fits the sequence of words $w_{1,n}$, while the first is simply the quantity we required from probabilistic language models.

Equation 2.11 is a programmatic description of the way in which a language model can influence a speech-recognition system. It may help to go down one level of detail to see how this might actually work. Suppose, for example, that the acoustic part of our system, after analyzing an early portion of a signal, decided that it contained three words, of which the first was one of a_1, a_2, a_3, the second one of b_1, b_2, and the third one of c_1, c_2, c_3, c_4. Furthermore, say that this portion of the system gives the probability that the signal could have arisen from these words—for example, it has values for terms like $P(a_2, b_1, c_4 \mid \text{speech signal})$. Ignoring these values for the moment, we could have the speech model then assign probabilities to all possible three-word sequences, such as $P(a_2, b_1, c_4)$. Once we know all of them we can take the products, for example

$$P(a_2, b_1, c_4)P(a_2, b_1, c_4 \mid \text{speech signal})$$

and the sequence of words that maximizes this is the one we want.

2.4 Entropy

The second claim we made for statistical models is that they have a ready-made figure of merit that can be used to compare models, the *per-word cross entropy* assigned to sample text. In the next few sections we work our way toward a definition of this term. We start in this section with the notion of *entropy*.

We approach the notion of entropy via coding theory. Suppose, to take a trivial example, you want to send a friend a message that is a number from 0 to 3. How long a message must you send? This question is not well-defined. If you can send decimal numbers then only one character is needed, while if only binary numbers can be used then two binary digits are required (as in 10 for the decimal number 2). To fix this, the standard is that all messages must be encoded in 0s and 1s, and message length is characterized by the number of *bits* required.

Now suppose you have to send messages of this form over and over. Perhaps you are watching a house with two occupants and every five minutes you need to send a message 0 = no occupants, 1 = first occupant in the house, 2 = second occupant in the house, and 3 = both occupants in the house. Now obviously you can send your two-bit message over and over, but can you do any better? Well, if all four messages are equally likely, then no, you cannot do any better. But suppose this is not the case; suppose we have the probabilities

Situation	Probability
No occupants	.5
1st occupant	.125
2nd occupant	.125
Both occupants	.25

The key idea in making a more efficient code is to use fewer bits for more frequent messages at the cost of more bits for the less frequent ones. In particular, a better code for these messages would be as follows:

Situation	Probability	Code
No occupants	.5	0
1st occupant	.125	110
2nd occupant	.125	111
Both occupants	.25	10

This kind of encoding is called a *variable-length encoding*, as different messages have codes of different lengths. To see that this is a legitimate code, we need to make sure that all the messages are handled (this is obvious) and that it can always be decided when one message ends and the next starts. This was obvious when all of the messages were of the same length, but may not be so clear now. The easiest way to see this is to construct a code tree, as in figure 2.1. We start at the top when the first message arrives. If a zero comes in, we go to the left. In this case we find a terminal node (with the decoded message) and thus we know that the message is over and that the next bit must start the next message. If we get a 1 we end up at a non-terminal node, and thus must wait for the next symbol. If the next is a 0, then we know that the message is "Both occupants" and that this message is over. In the same way we can decode, say, "111" as "Second occupant" and know that this message is over. From this tree it is easy to see that one can always tell when a message is over.

Furthermore, and this is the real point of this example, on the average this code requires fewer bits per message. To see this we simply note that for the half of the time when we get the "No occupants" message we need only one bit (for an average of $\frac{1}{2} \cdot 1$ bit $= \frac{1}{2}$ bit), that for a quarter of the time we need two bits for the "Both occupants" message ($\frac{1}{4} \cdot 2$ bits $= \frac{1}{2}$ bit), etc. The overall average is:

$$\frac{1}{2} \cdot 1\,\text{bit} + \frac{1}{4} \cdot 2\,\text{bits} + \frac{1}{8} \cdot 3\,\text{bits} + \frac{1}{8} \cdot 3\,\text{bits} = 1.75\,\text{bits} \qquad (2.12)$$

This coding trick can be used in a lot of situations. For English messages, one can think of each English letter as a new message to be encoded. Naturally one would find that the letters of the alphabet are not equally likely, and thus it would make a lot of sense to use fewer bits for the frequent letters (e.g., "a" and "e") and more bits for the less frequent ones (e.g., "x" and "z").

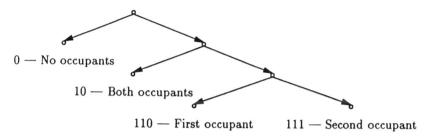

Figure 2.1
A code tree for number of occupants

In fact, a standard feature of the Unix operating system is a file compressor compress that uses a more sophisticated version of this scheme.

Now a message can be thought of as a random variable W that can take on one of several values $V(W)$ (four in the occupant example) and has a probability distribution P. Is there a lower bound on the number of bits needed to encode such a message (where again we are talking about how many bits are needed on the average if the message is sent many times)? The answer is yes, and the number is given by the *entropy* of a random variable, defined as:

$$H(W) \overset{\text{def}}{=} - \sum_{w \in V(W)} P(w) \log P(w) \tag{2.13}$$

where the log is log base two.

Consider our occupant problem again. For the probability distribution in that problem, the entropy of the message W_{occ} is:

$$H(W_{\text{occ}}) = - \left(\frac{1}{2} \cdot \log \frac{1}{2} + \frac{1}{4} \cdot \log \frac{1}{4} + \frac{1}{8} \cdot \log \frac{1}{8} + \frac{1}{8} \cdot \log \frac{1}{8} \right) \tag{2.14}$$

$$= - \left(\frac{1}{2} \cdot (-1) + \frac{1}{4} \cdot (-2) + \frac{1}{8} \cdot (-3) + \frac{1}{8} \cdot (-3) \right)$$

$$= 1.75$$

Note that the entropy comes out the same as the average number of bits per message. Furthermore, the parts of the sum in equation 2.12 are the same as those in equation 2.14 as well. This is not a complete coincidence. First, observe that the average number of bits to send a message W is given by

$$\sum_{w \in V(W)} P(w)\text{bits-required}(w) \tag{2.15}$$

Thus if we use $-\log P(w)$ bits to send the message w, the entropy and number of bits per message come out the same.

There are two important facts about the relation between entropy and encoding. The first is that the entropy of a message is the lower bound for the average number of bits needed to transmit that message. The second is that it is possible, in general, to get reasonably close to that minimum. The trick is to encode each individual message $w \in V(W)$ using (approximately) $\lceil -\log P(w) \rceil$ bits, where $\lceil x \rceil$ is the smallest integer greater than or equal to x. For example, consider the probability distribution for a message shown in figure 2.2. The code tree of figure 2.3 shows a variable-length encoding for this distribution that obeys all of the $\lceil -\log p \rceil$ numbers and lets us encode the message B in two bits rather than three.

We have said that the entropy of a message (viewed as a sequence of random variables) is a lower bound on the number of bits needed on the average to send the message. Alternatively, we can think of the entropy as a measure of our uncertainty about what a message says. If it takes a lot of bits to encode the message, we are quite uncertain; if only a few, we are more certain.

Consider speech recognition again. Reformulating equation 2.13 in terms of a sequence of words yields:

$$H(W_{1,n}) = - \sum_{w_{1,n} \in V(W_{1,n})} P(w_{1,n}) \log P(w_{1,n})$$

Just as we have taken to abbreviating $P(W_{1,n} = w_{i,n})$ as $P(w_{1,n})$, we also abbreviate $\sum_{w_{1,n} \in V(W_{1,n})}$ as $\sum_{w_{1,n}}$. Thus the previous equation becomes:

$$H(W_{1,n}) = - \sum_{w_{1,n}} P(w_{1,n}) \log P(w_{1,n})$$

The larger $H(W_{1,n})$, the harder the speech-understanding problem (all else equal). This is because our lesser ability to predict the next word gives less guidance to the entire system.

Note that entropy increases with the length of the message. Since most of the time we have no particular length in mind, a better measure of the difficulty of the recognition task is the *per-word* entropy, which is:

$$\frac{1}{n} H(W_{1,n}) = -\frac{1}{n} \sum_{w_{1,n}} P(w_{1,n}) \log P(w_{1,n}) \qquad (2.16)$$

Message	P(message)	$\lceil -\log p \rceil$	Message	P(message)	$\lceil -\log p \rceil$
A	.25	2	D	.13	3
B	.22	3	E	.125	3
C	.15	3	F	.125	3

Figure 2.2
A more complicated probability distribution for a message

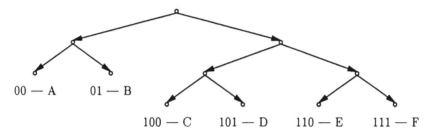

Figure 2.3
A more complicated code tree

For example, consider a speech-understanding system asked to transcribe random words picked with equal probabilities from the set {the, a, cat, dog, ate, slept, here, there}. Since each word is independent of the previous ones, the entropy for each word is:

$$H(W_1) = -P(\text{the}) \log P(\text{the}) - P(\text{a}) \log P(\text{a}) - \ldots - P(\text{there}) \log P(\text{there})$$
$$= 8 \cdot \left(-\frac{1}{8} \log \frac{1}{8} \right)$$
$$= 3$$

Actually, for our purposes the length of the message n is really a distraction, since we want to consider messages (texts) of many different, arbitrarily great lengths. Thus we often talk about $H(L)$, the *entropy of a language*, which is the limit of the per-word entropy as the length of message gets very large:

$$H(L) \overset{\text{def}}{=} - \lim_{n \to \infty} \frac{1}{n} \sum_{w_{1,n}} P(w_{1,n}) \log P(w_{1,n}) \tag{2.17}$$

Obviously, the language entropy of a sequence of words in which each word is chosen with equal probability from a set of eight possibilities is 3.

2.5 Markov Chains

Let us next consider a somewhat more English-like example. In this case we present the probabilistic model in the graphical format shown in figure 2.4. If we ignore the numbers on the arcs, this is the finite-state automaton one encounters in many computer-science courses. One starts at the start state (marked with →) and must end up at the final state (the double circle). In the automaton in figure 2.4, the initial and final states happen to be the same, but this need not be the case. Such automata can be thought as *acceptors*— machines that decide if an input is a member of a desired language (in which case the machine ends up in a final state)—or as *generators*—machines that can generate members of a desired language. In either case the symbols on the arcs are the terminal symbols used in the language. However, when one thinks of the automaton as an acceptor, one imagines that a string is externally supplied that then drives the automaton from state to state, following the arc labeled with the next symbol from the string. For example, the string "a dog slept" would drive the automaton in figure 2.4 from the starting state to the state on the right-hand side of the figure. If we think of the machine as a generator, then we can imagine the machine generating the string "a dog slept" by "randomly" choosing an arc and outputting the symbol found on the arc.

After adding the probabilities, we could call this a "probabilistic finite-state automaton," but such models have different names in the statistical literature. In particular, that in figure 2.4 is called a *Markov chain*. Like finite-state automata, Markov chains can be thought of as acceptors or generators. However, associated with each arc is the probability of taking that arc given that one is in the state at the tail of the arc. Thus the numbers associated with all of the arcs leaving a state must sum to one. The probability then of generating a given string in such a model is just the product of the probabilities of the arcs traversed in generating the string. Equivalently, as an acceptor the Markov chain assigns a probability to the string it is given. (This only works if all states are accepting states, something we assume for Markov processes.)

2.6 Cross Entropy

Now if our messages are generated by the automaton of figure 2.4, what is the per-word entropy? In fact, it is 1, since at each point there are only two

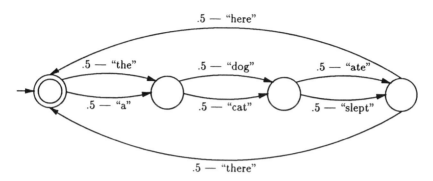

Figure 2.4
A trivial model of a fragment of English

equiprobable choices. This means, as should be intuitively clear, that this message is a lot less uncertain, and thus easier, than the one in which each of the eight output words was chosen at random. But suppose that, while the messages are in fact generated by this Markov chain, you do not know this and you design your speech-recognition system assuming each word was chosen at random. Then the structure would be doing your system no good since the system did not take advantage of it.

Our example is contrived, but the general situation is real. In dealing with real English we do not know the correct model (assuming for the sake of argument that there is a single "correct" model). Thus any model we use is, at best, only approximate. So we can ask, how much good does our approximate model do? One measure of this is given by the *cross entropy*. The cross entropy of a set of random variables $W_{1,n}$, where the correct model is $P(w_{1,n})$ but the probabilities are estimated using the model $P_M(w_{1,n})$, is given by:

$$H(W_{1,n}, P_M) \stackrel{\text{def}}{=} -\sum_{w_{1,n}} P(w_{1,n}) \log P_M(w_{1,n}) \tag{2.18}$$

Note that the cross entropy of a random variable according to the correct model is simply the random variable's entropy.

The *per-word cross entropy* is given by

$$\frac{1}{n}H(W_{1,n}, P_M) = -\frac{1}{n}\sum_{w_{1,n}} P(w_{1,n}) \log P_M(w_{1,n}) \tag{2.19}$$

It is left as an exercise for the reader to show that the cross entropy of the language defined in figure 2.4 using the random model is three bits/word. As a second example of the effects of the wrong model, consider the cross entropy when the correct model is that in figure 2.4 and the incorrect model is similar, except that the probabilities coming out of each node are not both .5, but one is instead .75 and the other .25. Then the cross entropy per word is about 1.2 bits.

As you can see, the incorrect model's cross entropy is larger than that of the correct model. Indeed, the entropy of a random variable is always less than its cross entropy according to an incorrect model. More formally,

$$H(W_{1,n}) \leq H(W_{1,n}, P_M) \tag{2.20}$$

with equality holding if and only if $P = P_M$. This suggests that one could compute the cross entropies of competing models and infer that the model with the smallest cross entropy is the best of the lot. In the cases we just looked at, the model that was intuitively closer to the correct model of figure 2.4 was ranked better by this metric.

Just as we defined the entropy of a language L by taking the limit as the length of the message grows, we can define the cross entropy of a language L given a model M as:

$$H(L, P_M) \stackrel{\text{def}}{=} - \lim_{n \to \infty} \frac{1}{n} \sum_{w_{1,n}} P(w_{1,n}) \log P_M(w_{1,n}) \tag{2.21}$$

2.7   Cross Entropy as a Model Evaluator

Unfortunately, in most cases we cannot use equation 2.21 to rank our models. As stated, calculating the cross entropy requires knowing the probabilities of seeing various English texts; that is, we need to know $P(w_{1,n})$. Fortunately, although this number is not available, we can estimate it by taking large representative samples of English text. In this case:

$$H(L, P_M) = - \lim_{n \to \infty} \frac{1}{n} \sum_{w_{1,n}} P(w_{1,n}) \log P_M(w_{1,n})$$

$$= - \lim_{n \to \infty} \frac{1}{n} \log P_M(w_{1,n}) \tag{2.22}$$

Formally, this holds if our language L is *ergodic*, a point we return to later.

A good way to understand this is to imagine that you are holding a contest for the best model of some process that is producing messages of length, say, 20 words, where each message is independent of the next. Obviously, if you know the correct probabilistic model, then evaluating the models presented to you is simply a matter of taking equation 2.19 and cranking out the per-word cross entropy for each model.

Suppose, however, that the probabilistic model is so simple that it has been given to you in the following form:

Message	Probability	Message	Probability
M1	.05	M5	.10
M2	.05	M6	.20
M3	.05	M7	.20
M4	.10	M8	.25

Given such a table we can, of course, continue to measure a model's cross entropy using equation 2.19. There is, however, a second option. Suppose we create a suite of 100 examples, five each of M1, M2, M3, ten each of M4 and M5, 20 each of M6 and M7, and 25 of M8, and apply equation 2.22 to get the cross entropy of the model. It is not hard to convince yourself that the results will be exactly those we got from equation 2.19. For example, consider the contribution of the probability the model assigns to message M1. According to equation 2.19 it is:

$$-\frac{1}{20} \cdot .05 \cdot \log P(\text{M1}) \tag{2.23}$$

On the other hand, for equation 2.22 we get:

$$-5 \cdot \frac{1}{20 \cdot 100} \cdot \log P(\text{M1}) \tag{2.24}$$

Here the 5 comes from the fact that M1 appears five times in the test data. Note how the probability of M1, .05, is exactly balanced by the 5/100 in equation 2.24. This happens for all of the messages, and hence the two equations give the same results.

The reason this works, of course, is that we were guaranteed in advance that the test suite of 100 examples was exactly indicative of the probabilistic model. In real life, as in dealing with English, there is no such perfect test suite. Nevertheless, it is not hard to make approximations to such a suite and use equation 2.22 with the understanding that the results of the model testing might be off because of biases in the suite. By the way, requiring that the language be "ergodic" is simply a fancy way to say that *any* sample of the language, if made long enough, is such a perfect sample.

It is worth pursuing our "competition" idea a bit further. Let us assume that you place no restrictions on the probabilistic models your contestants hand in. Furthermore, since the probabilistic model is not known to you, you have put together what you hope is a typical sample to test all of the models according to equation 2.21. Now suppose that one of the contestants is really a superhacker and, rather than bothering to figure out a probabilistic model, decides it would be easier to get hold of the data you intend to use for the evaluation. As there are no restrictions on the models, the hacker hands in a program that simply assigns probability one to your sample text and zero to everything else. This would certainly be cheating except that, since we made no restriction on the models and this is indeed a probabilistic model, albeit a rather trivial one, it could be argued that it was within the rules. If a lot of money was riding on the contest, the lawyers would have a field day.

The point here is that using equation 2.22 to measure the cross entropy of a model works only if the test sequence has not been used by the model builder. If it has, then it is possible to bias the model to fit the test, thus giving a false impression of the model's quality. Of course, in science the model builder is often the model tester as well, and the results of the test are included in reports on the model. In such cases one typically first creates a corpus, then randomly removes some of the data to be used for the test. The model is built on the basis of the rest of the data and then tested at the end on the reserved data. Generally the testing data is small compared to the training data—say 10% of the data for testing, the rest for training. When the model creation is automatic (i.e., no person need look at the training data to create the model), then a variation on this testing procedure is repeatedly to create and test the model, each time holding out a different 1/10th of the data, until all of the data has been used for testing in one of the sessions. This is called *cross validation*, and is one way to ensure that one's results are not an artifact of accidentally selecting some unrepresentative testing data.

Naturally, if your goal is to do well not simply on some scientific test but rather on, say, general English, then you need some source of "general English." One commonly used collection is the so-called "Brown corpus" developed by Francis and Kučera [20]. This contains slightly over a million words of text—the exact number depends on how you define a "word." In an effort to attain a representative sample of different kinds of English, the

Area	Segments
Press, reportage (political, sports, financial, etc.)	44
Press, editorial (including letters to the editor)	27
Press, reviews	17
Religion (books, periodicals, tracts)	17
Skills and hobbies (books, periodicals)	36
Popular lore (books, periodicals)	48
Belles lettres, biography, memoirs, etc.	75
Misc. (government, industry, college documents)	30
Learned (natural science, humanities, political sci.)	80

Figure 2.5
Coverage of the Brown corpus

corpus is composed of about 500 text segments, each of about 2000 words. Figure 2.5 gives some feel for how the segments are divided among different topics and purposes. All of the segments were first printed in the United States in 1961.

In talking about such language corpora one distinguishes between *word types* and *word tokens*. A word token is a particular occurrence of a word. Thus when we said that the Brown corpus had a million words, we could equally well have said that it had a million word tokens. Naturally, many of the million words are repeated, so one distinguishes between the million word tokens and the smaller number of word *types* (about 49,000, again depending on what you count as a word). There are other corpora of general English as well, although the Brown corpus is one of the earliest and probably the best known. Several of the programs we discuss in this book were developed and/or tested on this corpus.

By taking this or some other corpus we believe representative of the English our model is to handle (and is new material as far as our model is concerned), we can use equation 2.22 to give us a figure of merit for our model that can then be used to compare it to other language models. However, like any single number, we must treat this cross entropy with a great deal of caution. It is certainly possible for a model to produce a very good cross entropy yet not admit of extensions, while another, poorer according to our measure, suggests many improvements. It is like the old joke about the person trying to get to the moon by climbing the tallest tree. In such cases one might legitimately claim that one model is better for a production system while the other is the better research vehicle. We shall see such cases.

2.8 Exercises

2.1 Derive equation 2.8 by substituting in definitions.

2.2 What is the average number of bits required per message if we use the variable-length encoding in figure 2.3? Show that this is slightly larger than the entropy of the message described in figure 2.2.

2.3 Show that the cross entropy of the language described in figure 2.4 using a model in which all eight words are equally likely is three bits/word.

2.4 Show that the cross entropy of the language described in figure 2.4, using an incorrect model in which the transitions for "the," "dog," "ate," and "here" are assigned a probability of .75 and those for the other four words are assigned a probability of .25, is about 1.2 bits/word.

2.5 Prove equation 2.20 given the following inequality for real numbers:

$$\log x \leq x - 1 \tag{2.25}$$

where equality holds if and only if $x = 1$.

2.6 Using equation 2.20, prove that the entropy of a message W is a lower bound on the average number of bits required to send W.

3 Hidden Markov Models and Two Applications

One of the major pieces of intellectual machinery that has led to improved statistical language models is the notion of a *hidden Markov model* (HMM). In this chapter we consider two applications of hidden Markov models: trigram models of language and part-of-speech tagging.

3.1 Trigram Models of English

One of the least sophisticated but most durable of the statistical models of English is the n-gram model. This model makes the drastic assumption that only the previous $n - 1$ words have any effect on the probabilities for the next word. While this is clearly false, as a simplifying assumption it often does a serviceable job. A common n is three (hence the term *trigrams*). This means that:

$$P(w_n \mid w_1, \ldots, w_{n-1}) = P(w_n \mid w_{n-2}, w_{n-1}) \tag{3.1}$$

Thus the statistical language model becomes quite simple:

$$P(w_{1,n}) = P(w_1)P(w_2 \mid w_1)P(w_3 \mid w_{1,2}) \ldots P(w_n \mid w_{1,n-1}) \tag{3.2}$$

$$= P(w_1)P(w_2 \mid w_1)P(w_3 \mid w_{1,2}) \ldots P(w_n \mid w_{n-2,n-1}) \tag{3.3}$$

$$= P(w_1)P(w_2 \mid w_1) \prod_{i=3}^{n} P(w_i \mid w_{i-2,i-1}) \tag{3.4}$$

The first two terms simply take care of the probability of the first two words of $w_{1,n}$ (since we do not have two previous words upon which to condition the probability). To get rid of these terms in future equations, we assume that there are two "pseudo-words" w_{-1}, w_0 (which could be some "beginning-of-text" indicators) on which we can condition as well. This simplifies the equation to:

$$P(w_{1,n}) = \prod_{i=1}^{n} P(w_i \mid w_{i-2,i-1}) \tag{3.5}$$

To create such a model we simply go through some training text and record which pairs and triples of words appear in the text and how many times. Taking the last sentence as our training text, for instance, we would note the pair "(to, create)" and the triple "(to, create, such)," the pair "(create, such)," the triple "(create, such, a)," etc. We can then estimate the probabilities as follows, where $P_e(x)$ is the estimated probability for x based upon some counts C:

$$P_e(w_i \mid w_{i-2,i-1}) = \frac{C(w_{i-2,i})}{C(w_{i-2,i-1})} \tag{3.6}$$

So to estimate the probability that "such" appears after "to create" we count how many times the pair "to create" appears in our text and how many times "to create such" appears, and divide.

In chapter 2 we saw how to give a graphical representation of a probability distribution in terms of a Markov chain (see figure 2.4). Figure 3.1 shows a Markov chain for the trigram model of equation 3.5 in the case where there are only two symbols in the output vocabulary, "a" and "b." (We ignore the starting pseudo-words $w_{-1,0}$.) Each arc in the diagram represents a transition, and as such must indicate the output symbol as well as the probability of taking that arc. (For readability, the probabilities are shown for only some of the arcs.) One difference between this figure and figure 2.4 is that in 3.1 it is not possible to determine the state of the machine simply on the basis of the last output. It *is* possible on the basis of the last two outputs (i.e., the last two words), and thus one calls this a Markov chain of *order 2*. Readers should convince themselves that equation 3.5 and figure 3.1 assign the same probabilities to strings of "a"s and "b"s.

A major problem with our trigram model, and indeed one we encounter many times in this book, is that of *sparse data*. Suppose we collect the relevant statistics for our trigram model and then apply it to a new text in which a trigram occurs that never appeared in the training corpus. Equation 3.6 assigns a zero probability to the third word coming after the first two. Since $\log 0 = -\infty$, this gives the text a *very* poor cross entropy, and is obviously not what we want.

In fact, such things happen quite often. Jelinek [31] reports that after collecting statistics from a 1,500,000-word corpus and applying the resulting trigram model to a text of only 300,000 words, 25% of the trigrams in the second text did not appear in the first. (Jelinek does not specify, but one assumes he means that 25% of the trigram *types* are new. Presumably these are less common trigrams and thus account for only a small part of the approximately 300,000 trigrams in the smaller corpus. Or, to put it another way, the percentage in terms of *tokens* would be much smaller.) One solution to this problem is to "smooth" the probabilities by also using the bigram and unigram probabilities. That is, rather than equation 3.5, we instead use:

$$P(w_n \mid w_{n-2,n-1}) = \lambda_1 P_e(w_n) + \lambda_2 P_e(w_n \mid w_{n-1}) + \lambda_3 P_e(w_n \mid w_{n-2,n-1}) \tag{3.7}$$

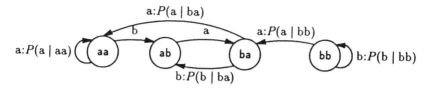

Figure 3.1
A Markov chain for trigrams

Here $\lambda_1, \lambda_2, \lambda_3$ are three nonnegative constants such that $\lambda_1 + \lambda_2 + \lambda_3 = 1$. If we assume that most of the time we do have trigrams and that they yield a more accurate assessment of the probabilities than bigrams or unigrams, then λ_3 should be so much higher than the other two that it dominates the probability calculations. Nevertheless, we should make $\lambda_3 < 1$ in order to allow the less precise probabilities to take over for missing trigrams. Since we could be missing bigrams also, we have included a unigram term.

Once we assign values to $\lambda_1, \lambda_2, \lambda_3$, such as, say, .1, .3, .6, and estimate the required probabilities by collecting statistics from a large corpus, we can then use equation 3.7 to assign better probabilities in that they are not zero when the relevant trigram or bigram data are missing.

Of course, where did the numbers .1, .3, .6 come from? It so happens the author just made up some numbers that seemed "reasonable." But are they? Would other numbers work better? One way to tell would be to try different numbers and see what cross entropy they assign to a new sample of text. This is possible, but it would clearly be better if we had an automatic way to find the best numbers, or at least pretty good numbers.

There is such a scheme for hidden Markov models (HMMs). HMMs are a generalization of Markov chains in which a given state may have several transitions out of it, all with the same symbol. (This is not allowed in Markov chains. There, from a given state, after a given symbol is output, only one next state is possible.) We wait until the next section of this chapter to define such models formally, preferring to start with an informal example.

So we want to turn equation 3.7 into an HMM, just as we turned the simpler version, equation 3.5, into the Markov chain of figure 3.1. This would let us apply the HMM parameter-adjustment scheme and we would be all set. Figure 3.2 shows a piece of such a model. The earlier version in figure 3.1 had an arc between nodes ab and ba (labeled "a") and between ab and bb (labeled "b"). These arcs have been replaced by the network in figure 3.2. Similar replacements would be necessary for the rest of the arcs in the simpler

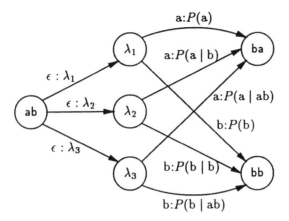

Figure 3.2
An HMM for the improved trigram model

model. Note that the arcs leading out of node ab all have for their output the symbol ϵ, the null output. We consider how to rid ourselves of these three ϵ-transitions shortly.

Looking more closely at figure 3.2 and comparing it to equation 3.7, we would like to convince ourselves that they define the same language model in that they assign the same probabilities to strings of the language. To do this we need to know one more fact about HMMs. Since more than one successor state may have the same output, in general there may be several paths through the HMM that produce the same output. It is easy to see this in figure 3.2. In such cases the probability of the output is the sum of the probabilities of all possible paths. The probability of a path is, as with Markov chains, the product of the probabilities of each transition in the path.

To convince ourselves that figure 3.2 and equation 3.7 assign the same probabilities, we first note superficially that equation 3.7 defines each conditional probability $P(w_i \mid w_{i-1,i-2})$ as a sum of three terms. In the same way, we can see that the HMM of figure 3.2 does the same thing since three paths through the HMM could have led to any given output, say "a," and the probability assigned to a string in an HMM is the sum over all possible paths through the HMM for that string.

Going down a level of detail, consider how a "b" might occur after outputting (or seeing) "ab." One way is that it could be output simply on account of the first term of the equation, $\lambda_1 P(w_i)$. This would correspond in figure 3.2 to taking the topmost arc from node ab to node λ_1 and then the arc from there to node bb. As we can see, this outputs a "b" and the probability of this sequence of arcs being followed (if we are at node ab) is $\lambda_1 P(b)$, just as in the equation. In the same way, a "b" could also occur by going first to node λ_2 and then to bb (with probability $\lambda_2 P(b \mid b)$) or by going to λ_3 and then to bb (with probability $\lambda_3 P(b \mid ab)$). The total probability of seeing a "b" after an "ab" would be the sum of these three, which is just what equation 3.7 says. So the HMM specifies the same probability as the equation.

As we noted earlier, figure 3.2 differs from our HMM model in that it contains ϵ-*transitions*, that is transitions with no corresponding output symbol. Fortunately, we can rid ourselves of this problem by simply pretending that the HMM actually outputs a special character e whenever it goes through an ϵ-transition. We then pretend that the observed sequence is not, say, "abbbab" but rather "eaebebebeaeb"—the original sequence with "e"s between every two symbols. Naturally we do not show this mess to the rest of the world.

3.2 Hidden Markov Models

We now define hidden Markov models more formally. An HMM is a four-tuple $< s^1, S, W, E >$ where S is a set of states, $s^1 \in S$ is the initial state of the model, W is a set of output symbols, and E is a set of edges or transitions. For each of the sets S, W, E we assume a canonical ordering of the elements:

$$S = < s^1, s^2, \ldots, s^\sigma > \tag{3.8}$$

$$W = < w^1, w^2, \ldots, w^\omega > \tag{3.9}$$

$$E = < e^1, e^2, \ldots, e^\epsilon > \tag{3.10}$$

(Note the difference in our notation between, say, w_i and w^i: w_i indicates the output (or input) at the ith time unit, whereas w^i is the ith element of the set W.) As indicated, the starting state of the HMM is the first element in the ordering of states. A transition is a four-tuple $< s^i, s^j, w^k, p >$, where $s^i \in S$ is the state the transition starts from, $s^j \in S$ is the state the transition takes us to, $w^k \in W$ is an output symbol that can be thought of as generated or accepted by the model depending on whether we are considering the model as an acceptor or generator of strings, and p is the probability of taking that transition. We frequently write such a transition thus: $s^i \xrightarrow{w^k} s^j$. No two transitions can have the same starting and ending states as well as the same output value. That is, there are no redundant transitions. As we are frequently interested in all possible sequences of states that the HMM can traverse, it makes things slightly easier to assume that our models have transitions for all possible outputs going to all possible next states. If we really do not want a certain transition, we can simply give it a zero probability. We feel free to leave out zero-probability paths in graphical representations of HMMs.

Note that a state a can be the starting state for several transitions that have the same output symbol but go to different ending states. Obviously in cases like this it is not possible to know what state the machine has gone into simply by looking at the output (or input if it is an acceptor). Thus the state sequence followed by an HMM is not deducible from the input. It is *hidden*.

We can think of the HMM as starting in state s^1. At time tick 1 it outputs (or accepts) w_1 and goes to state s_2. At time tick 2 it outputs w_2 and goes to state s_3. Thus at time tick n it outputs w_n and goes into s_{n+1}, so that there are $n + 1$ states for n outputs.

The probability p associated with a transition $s^i \xrightarrow{w^k} s^j$, $P(s^i \xrightarrow{w^k} s^j)$, is defined as the probability that at any time t the HMM outputs the tth symbol w^k and goes to the $(t + 1)$st state in the sequence of states, s^j, given that the tth state was s^i. (So at time t the HMM is in state s^i, and with probability p it outputs the tth symbol w^k and goes into the $(t + 1)$st state s^j.)

$$P(s^i \xrightarrow{w^k} s^j) \overset{\text{def}}{=} P(S_{t+1} = s^j, W_t = w^k \mid S_t = s^i) \quad 1 \le t \qquad (3.11)$$

$$= P(s^j, w^k \mid s^i) \qquad (3.12)$$

The second equation, 3.12, is an abbreviation we can use when it is understood that the state s^i is a state of the HMM just prior to the state s^j. Markov models assume that the only information affecting the probability of an output, or of the next state, is the prior state, as in equation 3.12. This is called the *Markov assumption*. More formally:

$$P(w_n, s_{n+1} \mid w_{1,n-1}, s_{1,n}) = P(w_n, s_{n+1} \mid s_n) = P(s^i \xrightarrow{w^k} s^j) \qquad (3.13)$$

To see how the Markov assumption figures in our calculations, let us look again at our earlier statement that the probability of a sequence $w_{1,n}$ is the probability of all possible paths through the HMM that can produce this sequence. In other words:

$$P(w_{1,n}) = \sum_{s_{1,n+1}} P(w_{1,n}, s_{1,n+1}) \qquad (3.14)$$

In equation 3.14, $s_{1,n+1}$ vary over all possible state sequences (with $s_1 = s^1$) since, as we noted earlier, we assume there are transitions from all states to every other state (and with all outputs), albeit some with zero probability. Given the Markov assumption of equation 3.13, we can then formally show how to compute the probabilities of sequences using our HMM:

$$P(w_{1,n}) = \sum_{s_{1,n+1}} P(w_{1,n}, s_{1,n+1}) \tag{3.15}$$

$$= \sum_{s_{1,n+1}} P(s_1)P(w_1, s_2 \mid s_1)P(w_2, s_3 \mid w_1, s_{1,2})$$

$$\dots P(w_n, s_{n+1} \mid w_{1,n-1}, s_{1,n}) \tag{3.16}$$

$$= \sum_{s_{1,n+1}} P(w_1, s_2 \mid s_1)P(w_2, s_3 \mid s_2) \dots P(w_n, s_{n+1} \mid s_n) \tag{3.17}$$

$$= \sum_{s_{1,n+1}} \prod_{i=1}^{n} P(w_i, s_{i+1} \mid s_i) \tag{3.18}$$

$$= \sum_{s_{1,n+1}} \prod_{i=1}^{n} P(s_i \xrightarrow{w_i} s_{i+1}) \tag{3.19}$$

Here equation 3.16 simply expands the probability equation using successive conditional probabilities. We simplify this in equation 3.17 by noting that the initial state s_1 is always the same and thus has probability one, and by using the Markov assumption of equation 3.13 on all of the conditional probabilities. Finally, equation 3.19 simply writes out the same thing more succinctly.

In chapter 4 we look at some algorithms for using HMMs. For example, while equation 3.19 states how to compute the probability of an output, it is not very useful since it frames the computation as a sum over all possible paths, and typically the number of possible paths grows exponentially with the length of the output string. In chapter 4 we develop a very efficient algorithm for doing this, as well as a very efficient algorithm for finding the most likely path that could produce a given output. Finally, we also give there the algorithm that adjusts HMM parameters (that is, the probabilities on the arcs) so that a given corpus is assigned a higher probability by the model. But first another application.

3.3   Part-of-Speech Tagging

In this section we consider a second application of HMMs—assigning part-of-speech tags to the words of a corpus. As we noted in chapter 1, many

English words can be in more than one part-of-speech class. Thus the problem of assigning part-of-speech tags is assigning the tags for such words. In this section we consider how to do this using an HMM.

Naturally, a major reason for using an HMM for this task is the automatic-training possibilities it provides. However, our techniques work only to improve the probability of the test corpus. In the trigram model we looked at earlier in this chapter, this was fine because we wanted to find parameters that enabled us to predict the input better. In part-of-speech tagging, however, the parameters we wish to improve are ones that assign parts of speech, not necessarily ones that assign probabilities to the input text. Nevertheless, if we are going to use the HMM's automatic-training ability we need to phrase the problem of assigning parts of speech to the words as one of assigning probabilities to the input text.

Well, HMMs have three things we can play with: the outputs, the transitions, and the states. We have just stated that the outputs must continue to be the words of the corpus for HMM training to be useful. Thus we have the states and the transitions. Suppose we assume that there is some connection between the states and the tags. Analogy with equation 3.14 suggests that we relate our parts of speech to the output text in the following fashion:

$$P(w_{1,n}) = \sum_{t_{1,n+1}} P(w_{1,n}, t_{1,n+1}) \tag{3.20}$$

Here $t_{1,n+1}$ is a sequence of $n + 1$ parts of speech or *tags*. We interpret this as n parts of speech for the n words plus a pointless prediction of a part of speech for the nonexistent w_{n+1}.

Formally, equation 3.20 is correct because we are summing over all possible, mutually exclusive $t_{1,n+1}$. Informally, equation 3.20 says that if we look at a corpus and find the percentage of time that $w_{1,n}$ is associated with some particular $t_{1,n+1}$, and we add that to the percentage of time that the same words appeared with some other sequence of part-of-speech tags, and we keep doing this until we have covered all possible assignments of parts of speech to those words, the result will be the probability of the words for any parts of speech—that is, the probability of the words.

The approach suggested by equation 3.20 looks even better when we define more precisely what we mean by assigning parts of speech. Formally we define the problem of part-of-speech tagging as finding

$$\arg\max_{t_{1,n}} P(t_{1,n} \mid w_{1,n}) = \arg\max_{t_{1,n}} \frac{P(w_{1,n}, t_{1,n})}{P(w_{1,n})} \tag{3.21}$$

$$= \arg \max_{t_{1,n}} P(w_{1,n}, t_{1,n}) \qquad (3.22)$$

where $\arg \max_x f(x)$ is the value of x that maximizes $f(x)$. So we want to find the $t_{1,n}$ that maximizes $P(t_{1,n} \mid w_{1,n})$. The term we wish to maximize in equation 3.22 also appears in equation 3.20, suggesting that the latter is on the right track. To make equation 3.22 into an HMM model, then, all that is left is to make explicit how the part-of-speech sequence relates to the state sequence.

There are several ways to relate parts of speech to states. Let us take the easiest and just say that each state in our HMM corresponds to the part of speech of the word produced next. An HMM with this assumption is shown in figure 3.3; we have simplified this figure by assuming only two parts of speech, n and v, and only two words, "a" and "b," and have left drawing the transitions from v to n as an exercise for the reader. The corresponding equations for our language model can be derived from equation 3.20 plus the assumption that the probability of a word appearing at a particular position given that its part of speech occurs at that position is independent of everything else, and that the probability of a part of speech coming next is dependent only on the previous part of speech. That is:

$$P(w_n \mid w_{1,n-1}, t_{1,n}) = P(w_n \mid t_n) \qquad (3.23)$$
$$P(t_n \mid w_{1,n-1}, t_{1,n-1}) = P(t_n \mid t_{n-1}) \qquad (3.24)$$

The resulting word-model equation is then:

$$P(w_{1,n}) = \sum_{t_{1,n+1}} P(w_{1,n}, t_{1,n+1}) \qquad (3.25)$$

$$= \sum_{t_{1,n+1}} \prod_{i=1}^{n} P(w_i \mid t_i) P(t_{i+1} \mid t_i) \qquad (3.26)$$

Given this or a similar language model, we can obtain the sequence of tags by finding the sequence of states that our HMM traversed in "producing" the output. Of course, we don't really know what this is, but as in equation 3.22 we can find the most likely sequence of parts of speech (= states) and take that as our answer. Chapter 4 gives an efficient algorithm for finding this most likely state sequence for an HMM.

There are, of course, other possible ways to relate parts of speech to states. If we assume that each state represents two parts of speech, that of the

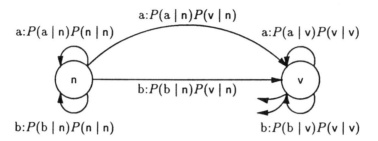

Figure 3.3
An HMM for word tagging

previous and current words, then we get a language model that looks like this:

$$P(w_{1,n}) = \sum_{t_{1,n+1}} \prod_{i=1}^{n} P(w_i \mid t_i) P(t_{i+1} \mid t_i, t_{i-1}) \tag{3.27}$$

It is also useful to consider some not-so-good language models to see why they are less desirable. For example, consider this model:

$$P(w_{1,n}) = \sum_{t_{1,n+1}} \prod_{i=1}^{n} P(w_i \mid t_i) P(t_{i+1} \mid t_i, w_i) \tag{3.28}$$

This differs from equation 3.26 in that the next part of speech is conditioned on not just the previous part of speech, but the previous word as well. In the abstract, including this dependence might or might not help the word model. In actuality, it is almost certainly a bad idea because of its effect on the sparse-data problem. For example, consider the word "blueberry." It occurs only twice in the Brown corpus (counting the single occurrences of both "blueberry" and "blueberries"), so to a first approximation its prior probability is something like $5 \cdot 10^{-6}$. Now consider the probability that a conjunction (e.g., and, or, but) comes after it. There are about 37,000 conjunctions in the Brown corpus. Assume that, say, 20,000 of these come after nouns and that "blueberry" is no more or less likely to have one than any other noun. Furthermore, assume that all occurrences of "blueberry" are nouns. Now, consider what this means for the counts upon which we make our probability estimates:

$$P_e(\text{conj} \mid W_{t-1} = \text{blueberry}, t_{t-1} = \text{noun}) = \frac{C(\text{blueberry, conj})}{C(\text{blueberry})} \tag{3.29}$$

But if the above assumptions are right, "blueberry" is followed by a conj only about once in 10^7 ($= 1/(5 \cdot 10^{-6} \times 2 \cdot 10^{-2})$) words. So even in a comparatively large corpus of ten million words one might not see this combination, in which case the counts one gets would be badly off. The point then is that in such models one must be careful not to introduce conditioning events (like the particular word) unless one has a *very* good reason for doing so, as they can make the data even sparser than necessary.

The better models typically perform at about the 95% level of correctness [13,16,18,31]: that is, about one word in twenty is given the wrong part of speech. How good or bad this is is largely a matter of one's preconceptions. Many people believe that most English words belong to only one part of speech, and thus that even the dumbest model ought to work just fine. This, however, is not the case. For example, consider the sentence "I drove home." The dictionary states that "I" is both a noun and a pronoun, "drove" is both a noun and a verb, and "home" is a noun, verb, and adjective. Furthermore, rather than the ten or so parts of speech considered in chapter 1, tagging programs typically deal with 40 or more parts of speech, making ambiguity more common. For a less anecdotal idea of how hard the problem really is, we can turn to the Brown corpus mentioned briefly in chapter 2. The Brown corpus was tagged by hand—that is, people sat down and assigned tags to each word on the basis of their intuitions—and thus it is possible to get a good idea of how many tags there are for each of the words in the corpus. The information in figure 3.4 is taken from DeRose [18]. As we can see, only about 11% of the word types in the Brown corpus are ambiguous with regard to the tags they take. On the other hand, these tend to be very common words; in fact, over 40% of the word tokens are ambiguous.

So 95% sounds pretty good, or at least until one is told yet another statistic. Consider a really simpleminded program that just assigns to each word its most likely part of speech c—that is, the one that maximizes $P(c \mid w)$. This program gets about 91% correct [13]. So perhaps the problem is not so hard after all.

Either way, there have been several programs that tag words more or less in the way we have described [16,18,31]. The work by Jelinek [31] is the closest to what is described in this section. In fact, the only difference is that Jelinek's work is based upon a trigram part-of-speech model rather than the bigram model used in equation 3.26. The work by Church [16] and DeRose [18] both differ more dramatically from our exposition. First, neither of the programs uses the training procedure for HMMs; they rather collect the statistical information from the hand-tagged Brown corpus. With the database

Number of tags	Number of word types
1 tag	35340
2 tags	4100
3 tags	264
4 tags	61
5 tags	12
6 tags	2
7 tags	1

Figure 3.4
Tag ambiguity in the Brown corpus; the word with seven tags is "still"

created in such a process it is easy directly to compute the parameters needed for equation 3.26. The programs also differ from our account in exactly the statistical parameters used. Church makes part-of-speech predictions based upon trigrams, but starts from the end of the sentence and works backward; DeRose uses the bigram model starting at the front of the sentence.

Interestingly, Church and DeRose cite a different figure of merit that they try to maximize. The figure of merit maximized in equation 3.26 is:

$$\prod_{i=1}^{n} P(w_i \mid t_i) P(t_{i+1} \mid t_i) \tag{3.30}$$

That is, the $t_{1,n}$ that maximizes the term of equation 3.30 is deemed the correct one. For DeRose, on the other hand, the term to maximize is:

$$\prod_{i=1}^{n} P(t_i \mid w_i) P(t_{i+1} \mid t_i) \tag{3.31}$$

Note the difference between $P(t_i \mid w_i)$ and $P(w_i \mid t_i)$. Church's paper also uses the term in equation 3.31, except that he uses a trigram model and works from back to front of the sentence. However, Church in a personal communication states that this was a mistake: the results of his paper were achieved using equation 3.30, not equation 3.31, and the latter gave him consistently poorer results. Boggess et al. [6] picked up on this difference, tried both, and reported the opposite results. However, they experimented only on very small corpora and their accuracies using the two methods were only 84% and 89%, rather than the more common 95% achieved using larger amounts of training data. To settle this point, Charniak et al. [13] tried both on the Brown corpus, training on 90% of the sentences and testing on the remaining 10%. Using the full Brown corpus tag set, which had 471 distinct tags, they found that the theoretically purer equation 3.30 did significantly better, 95.04% vs. 94.09% for the less pure equation 3.31. (In this test any difference over .1% would be statistically significant at the 95% level.)

3.4 Exercises

3.1 Why must $\lambda_1, \lambda_2, \lambda_3$ in equation 3.7 sum to 1?

3.2 Although we did not indicate it, the λs of equation 3.7 can, in principle, vary for different $w_{i-2,i-1}$. Explain why the λs can be a function of $w_{i-2,i-1}$ but not of w_i.

3.3 What should the probabilities be for the two incomplete arcs in figure 3.3?

3.4 Consider a part-of-speech tagger that bases its prediction of the next part of speech not just on the previous one, but on the previous two. Sketch the HMM for this model.

3.5 Formally state the Markov assumptions that lie behind equation 3.27 and then derive this equation from them.

3.6 In deriving equation 3.5 we noted the need to define the pseudo-words w_{-1} and w_0. One possibility mentioned there was to create a new beginning-of-text word for this purpose. However, this can create problems, especially if we smooth using terms like $P(w_i)$ and $P(w_i \mid w_{i-1})$. Can you think what difficulties might arise? There is a way of defining w_{-1} and w_0 without introducing a new pseudo-word, and this method solves the problems to which we just alluded. How is this done?

3.7 Another way to smooth the trigram language model of equation 3.5 would be to combine the trigram model with the part-of-speech model so that the probability of a word would depend not just on the previous words, but also on our prediction of its part of speech. In this exercise we develop equations for such a model.

(a) Derive an equation for $P(w_{1,n})$ that also uses $t_{1,n}$. Do not make any independence assumptions. The result should be of the same form as equation 3.2.

(b) Formalize the following two Markov assumptions: the probability of a word given all previous parts of speech and words is dependent only on the last part of speech and the two previous words, and the probability of a part of speech given the previous words and parts of speech is dependent only on the previous part of speech. Use these two assumptions to simplify the equation from (a).

(c) The equation you get in (b) will have one significant term that must be smoothed: $P(w_i \mid w_{i-2,i-1}, t_i)$. Write an equation for this term that looks like equation 3.7.

A language model of this form has, in fact, been implemented. Jelinek [30] describes such a model but reports that the improvement over the smoothed trigram model was too modest to offset the added complexity of the program.

3.8 We noted that Church [16] based his tagging model on predicting the part of speech t_i on the basis of the parts of speech that *followed* rather than preceded it. In fact, this in general has no effect on the results. In particular, show that for a bigram part-of-speech model, going both ways produces exactly the same answer if we assume that a special tag, t^0, is added to the front and back of the sequence and that this tag appears nowhere else. Show the same is true for a n-gram part-of-speech model if we add $n - 1$ t^0s to the front and back.

3.9 Write a program that collects trigram, bigram, and unigram statistics on a corpus of English text. Write a second program that takes these statistics plus a new corpus and sees how often tag trigrams appear that were not in the first corpus. Write a program that computes the probability of a corpus, using equation 3.7 for the conditional probabilities. Try the program for different values of the λs.

3.10 Write a program that takes a corpus of tagged English text (possibly generated from a simple grammar using the program in exercise 1.7) and collects the statistics needed to estimate $P(w_i \mid t_i)$ and $P(t_{i+1} \mid t_i)$, as in equation 3.30. Next write a program to compute the path through an HMM that maximizes this equation.

4 Algorithms for Hidden Markov Models

In the last chapter we developed HMM models for two problems. The first was to estimate the probability of English text using a "smoothed" trigram model. We need to smooth because training text often provides inaccurate counts for less common trigrams (often zero, when in fact they can and do occur in normal text). The smoothing was accomplished by adding terms for bigrams and unigrams into the probability assignment with weighting factors λ_1, λ_2, and λ_3. We then noted that HMMs have a way of automatically improving the values assigned to such parameters, in that the new values typically make the text more probable (and never make it less probable). Of course, to use such a model after we have found the parameters, we need to be able to determine the probability the HMM assigns to any particular output. Furthermore, for our second problem, the part-of-speech tagger, we also needed a way to find the most likely path through an HMM given a particular input $w_{1,n}$ (the path corresponding to the most likely tags for the sentence).

This chapter develops the algorithms used in such applications. We first see how to find efficiently the most likely path through an HMM, then we derive some efficient algorithms for assigning probabilities to strings produced by an HMM, and finally we develop the algorithm for doing the training.

4.1 Finding the Most Likely Path

In this section we develop the *Viterbi algorithm* [42] for finding the most likely path through an HMM given a particular output sequence. That is, for a string of length n this algorithm finds $\sigma(n+1)$, which is defined as follows:

$$\sigma(t) \stackrel{\text{def}}{=} \arg \max_{s_{1,t}} P(s_{1,t} \mid w_{1,t-1}) \tag{4.1}$$

$$= \arg \max_{s_{1,t}} P(s_{1,t}, w_{1,t-1}) \tag{4.2}$$

We actually use the form in equation 4.2, which simply omits the scaling factor $1/P(w_{1,n})$. Since the words stay the same, they serve only to ensure that the states are in fact the best states for those words (as opposed to some other string of the same length).

This algorithm is actually pretty simple. The basic idea is to compute the most likely state sequence starting with the empty output sequence, working up to the answer one output at a time. At each stage one need only compute

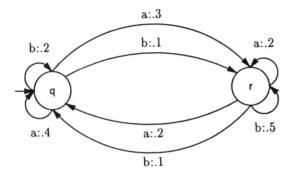

Figure 4.1
A simple HMM

	States	ϵ	b	bb	bbb	bbba
q	sequence	q	qq	qqq	qqqq	qrrrq
	probability	1.0	.2	.04	.008	.005
r	sequence	r	qr	qrr	qrrr	qrrrr
	probability	0.0	.1	.05	.025	.005

Figure 4.2
Most likely state sequences

the most likely sequence (and its probability) that ends in state s^i for all states. Consider the HMM in figure 4.1. The table in figure 4.2 shows, for each input, the most likely sequences (and their probabilities) that could lead to each possible state. The input in question is "bbba." Figure 4.3 shows another way of viewing the search for the best path. It indicates what state sequences need be considered as the HMM progresses through the input (shown on the right). The reader may want to consult both figures 4.2 and 4.3 in the course of the following discussion.

We start with the empty string ϵ. As indicated, the best state sequence that ends in state q is just q, and this sequence has probability 1, since q is the starting state. Naturally, the best sequence that ends in r is just r, but it has probability 0, since no sequence can start in state r.

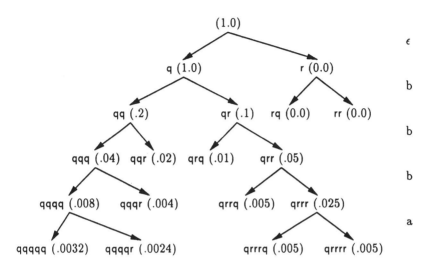

Figure 4.3
An alternate view of the search for the best path

Next consider the best sequences after just the input "b." There are two ways to end up in state q after seeing a "b." The obvious one is to start from q and take the upper left-hand arc in figure 4.1 back to q. The resulting probability—that is, the probability of the best path to q times the probability from there back to q—is $1 \times .2 = .2$. The other path to q after seeing just a "b" would be from state r, but since the best path to r at this point has probability zero, clearly the best way to end up at q at this point cannot be through r. Thus the best sequence to get to q after "b" is qq. In just the same way, the best way to end up at r after "b" is qr.

Next the algorithm would consider the best ways to end up at each of the states after "bb." There are again two ways to end up at q. We could be at q at the last time tick and stay there. This path has a best-path probability equal to the best probability for getting to q at the last time tick times the probability of outputting a "b" and staying there, or $.2 \times .2 = .04$. The other way of being at q is to come there from r, for a probability of $.1 \times .1 = .01$. So the best way to be at q after "bb" is via path qqq. By the same sort of calculation we can find that the best way to end up at r after "bb" is to have been at r and stayed there.

Note that for each time tick it is necessary to store the best path and its probability *for each possible state*. Just storing the overall best path is not sufficient. For example, the most probable path that produces the string "b" is qq, but this is not a sub-path of of qrr, the most probable path for the string "bb". Had we not stored the path and probability associated with qr, we would have been unable to discover the more probable qrr. On the other hand, and this is the key point, you need nothing more than the best paths to each state (and the associated probability). For example, note in figure 4.3 that we never need consider more than four paths of any length. The best way to end up at q at some time tick must come from either q or r. In either case, the best way to have gotten to that place (q or r) remains the same, as does its probability, and obviously there can be no point in having taken a second-best path there. This is why we can find the best path in linear, not exponential, time.

Let us now say this more formally. Let $\sigma_i(t)$ be the state sequence that has maximum probability of generating $w_{1,t-1}$ (or one such sequence if there is a tie) and ends up in state s^i:

$$\sigma_i(t) \stackrel{\text{def}}{=} \arg \max_{s_{1,t}} P(w_{1,t-1}, s_{1,t-1}, S_t = s^i) \tag{4.3}$$

From this definition and equation 4.2 we can see how to use $\sigma_i(t)$ to get the sequence we want—just consider $\sigma_i(n+1)$ for all i and pick the one with the highest probability. Given this definition, the above example demonstrates the following:

$$\sigma_i(1) = s^i \tag{4.4}$$

$$\sigma_i(t+1) = \sigma_j(t) \circ s^i, \qquad j = \arg \max_{k=1}^{\sigma} P(\sigma_k(t)) P(s^k \stackrel{w_t}{\to} s^i) \tag{4.5}$$

Here $\circ$ indicates concatenation. Equation 4.5 is the crucial one since it states that, once we know the best ways to get to all states at time t, then the best way to get to a state at $t+1$ is a simple extension of one of those.

It is also possible to use the same algorithm to work backward from the end of the output/state sequence to the beginning. Let $\gamma_i(t)$ be a state sequence with the maximum probability of generating $w_{t,n}$ while starting in state s^i. In exactly the same way we get these equations:

$$\gamma_i(n+1) = s^i \tag{4.6}$$

$$\gamma_i(t-1) = s^i \circ \gamma_j(t), \qquad j = \arg \max_{k=1}^{\sigma} P(s^i \stackrel{w_{t-1}}{\to} s^k) P(\gamma_k(t)) \tag{4.7}$$

4.2 Computing HMM Output Probabilities

Next we give two ways of computing the probability of any particular HMM output (or, equivalently, the probability that the HMM assigns to any input). Both algorithms are much like the Viterbi algorithm for finding the most likely sequence of states given the output. The first is particularly similar in that it also incrementally computes probabilities for the output on a word-by-word basis, starting from the first word. The second algorithm is the mirror image of the first in that it computes the probability starting from the end of the output sequence and working toward the beginning. This second one is of no particular interest in its own right, but is needed for the HMM training algorithm.

Let $\alpha_i(t)$ be the probability of producing $w_{1,t-1}$ while ending up in state s^i. That is,

$$\alpha_i(t) \overset{\text{def}}{=} P(w_{1,t-1}, S_t = s^i), \qquad t > 1 \tag{4.8}$$

For $t = 1$ we can think of $w_{1,0}$ as the empty string, in which case the following definition makes sense:

$$\alpha_i(1) \overset{\text{def}}{=} \begin{cases} 1.0 & \text{if } i = 1 \\ 0 & \text{otherwise} \end{cases} \tag{4.9}$$

This incorporates the fact that we must start in state s^1.

The quantity $\alpha_i(t)$ is called the *forward probability* and is significant for two reasons. First, it is easy to compute $P(w_{1,n})$ if we have all of the $\alpha_i(n+1)$s, and second, we can compute the $\alpha_i(t)$s in linear time by working *forward* through the entire output sequence, word by word.

For the first of these claims, we simply note that

$$P(w_{1,n}) = \sum_{i=1}^{\sigma} P(w_{1,n}, S_{n+1} = s^i) \tag{4.10}$$

$$= \sum_{i=1}^{\sigma} \alpha_i(n+1) \tag{4.11}$$

Next we show how to compute the $\alpha_i(t)$s starting from the $\alpha_i(1)$s and working forward to the $\alpha_i(n+1)$s. We do this recursively. The base step comes directly from the definition of $\alpha_i(t)$ in equation 4.9. Next we show how to compute $\alpha_j(t + 1)$ if we know all the $\alpha_j(t)$s:

$$\alpha_j(t + 1) = P(w_{1,t}, S_{t+1} = s^j)$$

$$= \sum_{i=1}^{\sigma} P(w_{1,t}, S_t = s^i, S_{t+1} = s^j)$$

$$= \sum_{i=1}^{\sigma} P(w_{1,t-1}, S_t = s^i)P(w_t, S_{t+1} = s^j \mid w_{1,t-1}, S_t = s^i)$$

$$= \sum_{i=1}^{\sigma} P(w_{1,t-1}, S_t = s^i)P(w_t, S_{t+1} = s^j \mid S_t = s^i)$$

$$= \sum_{i=1}^{\sigma} \alpha_i(t)P(s^i \xrightarrow{w_t} s^j) \tag{4.12}$$

Steps two and three here are standard probability theory, step four applies the Markov assumption, and the last step inserts definitions. Figure 4.4 uses the resulting equation 4.12 to calculate the $\alpha_i(t)$s for the HMM of figure 4.1 on the input "bbba." The top line gives the ts for the $\alpha_i(t)$s. Note that since $\alpha_i(t)$ takes into account the output only up to $t - 1$, the time-tick number is always one larger than the number of outputs. For example, the first output, "b," is at time tick 2 because it is $\alpha_i(2)$ that accounts for the first output. As calculated in figure 4.4, the probability of that sequence is .0279 in our model.

The quantity $\alpha_i(t)$ is called the *forward* probability because it (in effect) calculates the probability by moving forward in the sequence. In this respect it is like our first method of finding the most probable state sequence. And, just as in this other problem, it is also possible to calculate the probability of a sequence by working backward from the end, using a related quantity called the *backward probability*. This in itself is not particularly useful, unless for some reason working backward is easier for your problem, but since backward probabilities are also used in HMM training we introduce them here.

A backward probability $\beta_i(t)$ is the probability of seeing the sequence $w_{t,n}$ if the state of the HMM at time t is s^i:

$$\beta_i(t) \overset{\text{def}}{=} P(w_{t,n} \mid S_t = s^i) \tag{4.13}$$

Time ticks	1	2	3	4	5
Input	ϵ	b	bb	bbb	bbba
$\alpha_q(t)$	1.0	.2	.05	.017	.0148
$\alpha_r(t)$	0.0	.1	.07	.04	.0131
$P(w_{1,t})$	1.0	.3	.12	.057	.0279

Figure 4.4
The forward probabilities of "bbba"

As already mentioned, backward probabilities can be used to calculate the overall probability of a sequence:

$$\beta_1(1) = P(w_{1,n} \mid S_1 = s^1) \tag{4.14}$$
$$= P(w_{1,n}) \tag{4.15}$$

Also, just as with forward probabilities, we can calculate $\beta_i(t)$ starting from the end of the output sequence and working our way backward, at each step calculating the $\beta_i(t)$s for all states s^i. For the base step, we simply note that the probability of producing ϵ given that one is going to produce a string of length zero is 1, whatever state one is in. Thus we get:

$$\beta_i(n+1) = P(\epsilon \mid S_{n+1} = s^i)$$
$$= 1 \tag{4.16}$$

Next we consider the recursive step:

$$\beta_i(t-1) = P(w_{t-1,n} \mid S_{t-1} = s^i) \tag{4.17}$$
$$= \sum_{j=1}^{\sigma} P(w_{t-1,n}, S_t = s^j \mid S_{t-1} = s^i)$$
$$= \sum_{j=1}^{\sigma} P(w_{t-1}, S_t = s^j \mid S_{t-1} = s^i) P(w_{t,n} \mid w_{t-1}, S_t = s^j, S_{t-1} = s^i)$$
$$= \sum_{j=1}^{\sigma} P(w_{t-1}, S_t = s^j \mid S_{t-1} = s^i) P(w_{t,n} \mid S_t = s^j)$$

$$= \sum_{j=1}^{\sigma} P(s^i \overset{w_{t-1}}{\to}{}^1 s^j)\beta_j(t) \tag{4.18}$$

In this derivation the first two steps are again standard probability theory, the next step uses the Markov assumption, and the final step inserts $\beta_i(t)$ and $P(s^i \overset{w_{t-1}}{\to}{}^1 s^j)$ for their definitions. Figure 4.5 shows the calculation of P(bbba) using equation 4.18. The value of $\beta_q(1)$ is the same as that of $P(w_{1,4})$ in figure 4.4, as it should be. We did not bother to calculate $\beta_r(1)$, as it plays no role in the calculation of the probability for the sequence.

4.3   HMM Training

We are now in a position to give the training algorithm for HMMs, sometimes called the *forward-backward algorithm* or the *Baum-Welch algorithm* [5]. More precisely, we develop here an algorithm that, given a training sequence, adjusts the HMM parameter probabilities to make that training sequence as likely as possible. Thus if the training sequence is a representative one, it should improve the HMM's behavior on other sequences as well. Of course, if the HMM had enough states (and the right structure), the best way to make the training sequence as likely as possible would be to "memorize" it and assign it a probability of one. In practice, of course, our training text is much larger than the number of states in the HMM so memorization is not possible.

To start, let us consider a particularly simple case. Suppose we have not a true HMM but a Markov chain. With a Markov chain, given the output it is possible to follow the chain from state to state throughout the sequence. Now suppose someone gives you some representative text created by this Markov chain. You are also given the chain, but the probabilities on the arcs are missing. Is it possible to estimate what those probabilities should be? Clearly yes, and by a very simple algorithm. One simply goes through the text, noting whenever a transition t is taken during the processing of the training text. Then the estimated probability of taking transition t that leaves from state s is the number of times t was taken divided by the number of times any transition out of s was taken. For example, consider the Markov chain in figure 4.6. Suppose our training text is "abbaababbaaa." When we follow this through the chain, we find that the transitions were used the number of times indicated in figure 4.7. So, for example, $P_e(q \overset{a}{\to} r) = 5/8$, while $P_e(q \overset{b}{\to} q) =$

	1	2	3	4	5
	bbba	bba	ba	a	ϵ
$\beta_q(i)$	.0279	.063	.18	.7	1
$\beta_r(i)$		.153	.27	.4	1

Figure 4.5
The backward probabilities of "bbba"

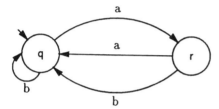

Figure 4.6
Markov chain lacking transition probabilities

3/8. More formally, let C be a function from transitions to estimates on the number of times the transition is used in a training corpus:

$$P_e(s^i \xrightarrow{w^k} s^j) = \frac{C(s^i \xrightarrow{w^k} s^j)}{\sum_{l=1,m=1}^{\sigma,\omega} C(s^i \xrightarrow{w^m} s^l)} \tag{4.75}$$

Thus there is a simple algorithm for estimating the parameters for a Markov chain. The algorithm for HMMs is conceptually the same, though more complicated in execution. We still use equation 4.19 to estimate the transition probabilities; what changes is how we obtain the transition counts. We cannot simply follow the HMM from state to state, since in general there are many paths the HMM could have taken to produce the output and we do not know which transitions were actually used.

Two key ideas are needed to solve this problem. The first is that when we cannot be sure which transition was used, we simply pretend that they were all used but prorate them according to the probability of the path in which the arc appears. That is, suppose we have two paths through our test corpus,

arc from	arc to	arc output	count
q	r	a	5
q	q	b	3
r	q	a	2
r	q	b	2

Figure 4.7
Counts on transitions for a Markov chain

one of which has probability 1/3 and the other 2/3. Transition a was used in the first whereas transition b was used in the second. Using the prorating idea, we would give transition a a count of 1/3 and b a count of 2/3. If b was used twice in the second path it would get a count of 4/3. Thus to get the total count for a transition we look at each path, count how many times the transition was used in the path, multiply it by the path's probability (to prorate it) and sum over all paths. More formally, we define the count function C as:

$$C(s^i \xrightarrow{w^k} s^j) = \sum_{s_{1,n+1}} P(s_{1,n+1} \mid w_{1,n}) \eta(s^i \xrightarrow{w^k} s^j, s_{1,n}, w_{1,n}) \qquad (4.20)$$

$$= \frac{1}{P(w_{1,n})} \sum_{s_{1,n+1}} P(s_{1,n+1}, w_{1,n}) \eta(s^i \xrightarrow{w^k} s^j, s_{1,n}, w_{1,n}) \qquad (4.21)$$

Here $\eta(s^i \xrightarrow{w^k} s^j, s_{1,n}, w_{1,n})$ counts the number of times $s^i \xrightarrow{w^k} s^j$ appears in the state sequence $s_{1,n+1}$ when the output is $w_{1,n}$. Note that when there is only one path, equation 4.21 reduces to the simple algorithm of just counting the number of times each transition is used in the course of processing $w_{1,n}$.

Now before we confront the total problem of computing the probabilities of taking a transition, we must deal with one small but important aspect of it. *Computing the path probabilities surely requires knowledge of the transition probabilities.* That is, if we already have the probabilities for our HMM, then clearly we can compute the path probabilities needed in equation 4.21 (even if the number of paths is exponential and it takes a long time). But without

Old_Cross_Entropy = 0.0
Guess HMM parameters
New_Cross_Entropy = Re-estimate_Parameters()
Loop until (Old_Cross_Entropy ≈ New_Cross_Entropy)
        Old_Cross_Entropy = New_Cross_Entropy
        New_Cross_Entropy = Re-estimate_Parameters()
End Loop

Figure 4.8
Top-level algorithm for HMM training

such numbers it is hard to imagine how we could compute anything. So it would appear that we need to *have* the transition probabilities before we can *estimate* the transition probabilities.

Enter at this point the second key idea. We make a guess at the HMM parameters and use this guess to compute the probabilities required in equation 4.21. These counts are used to re-estimate the parameters according to equation 4.19. We then use these new values for the probabilities to get new counts by processing the training corpus all over again. We continue this process until the probabilities settle down. We can wait either until none of the transition probabilities changes much from one iteration to the next or until the probability assigned to the training corpus does not change much. We do the latter since it is slightly simpler: we show that our algorithm computes that number anyway, and it is easier to compare two numbers (the old and new $P(w_{1,n})$) than two vectors of numbers (the old and new HMM parameters). Also, we calculate the per-word cross entropy of the corpus rather than the probability, as that is the figure of merit we recommended in chapter 2. The broad outline of our HMM training procedure is given in figure 4.8. We assume there that the parameter re-estimation routine returns the per-word cross entropy.

It may not be obvious to the reader that this algorithm works, or even does anything meaningful at all. We do not prove here that it works; for this the reader may consult [5, 32]. Rather, let us try to get some intuitions about it. Consider the HMM of figure 4.9(a). Our goal is to infer its parameters. As an initial guess we use the parameters of figure 4.9(b). We will see how the training algorithm can fix up the incorrect probabilities of the (b) version. To keep things simple, we take the training sequence to be "01011". Four possible paths could produce this output: ababaa, abaaaa, aaabaa, and

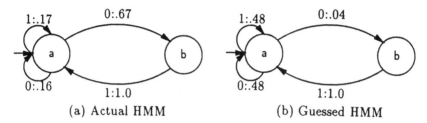

Figure 4.9
Two similar HMMs with different probabilities

aaaaaa. That is, the first two "01" sequences could be produced by either an ab path or an aa path, and the final "1" must be a aa path. Figure 4.10 shows the calculations for two iterations of the algorithm in figure 4.8. (We have simplified the calculations somewhat by omitting the $1/P(w_{1,5})$ term of equation 4.21. We can do this because we are interested in the counts from equation 4.21 only insofar as they let us calculate improved probabilities using equation 4.19. But in that equation the counts (and thus the term $1/P(w_{1,5})$) appear in both the numerator and denominator, so a constant term $1/P(w_{1,5})$ thereby cancels out. Thus we can ignore it when calculating the counts.) Next to each path in figure 4.10 we give first the probability assigned to the path according to the current transition probabilities (starting with those of figure 4.9(b)) and then the prorated numbers that the path adds to the counts for each of the transitions. Below the line we sum the counts and the probabilities of all of the paths. The reader should note that initially the probability assigned to the string is .035, and after the first recalculation it is .042. While we do not show it in figure 4.10, after the second retraining the probability is .047 (so, indeed, the new HMM parameters assign a higher probability to the training sequence). After the totals we give the rounded totals, which are the numbers used in further calculations. We also give the sum of the counts for all of the transitions out of state a (in the column $\sum a \xrightarrow{w} s$), since that is needed to recalculate the new probabilities for those transitions that leave a (see equation 4.19). We then use the rounded counts to compute the new probabilities for each of the transitions. Note how the probability for the transition $a \xrightarrow{0} b$ increases at each iteration, continuing to do so until it reaches something like the correct probability (within the limits of this artificially short and not-quite-representative training sequence).

The basic idea of figure 4.10 is that, despite the low probabilities initially assigned to the transition $a \xrightarrow{0} b$, the comparatively large number of outputs

Path	$P(Path)$	$a \xrightarrow{0} b$	$b \xrightarrow{1} a$	$a \xrightarrow{0} a$	$a \xrightarrow{1} a$	$\sum a \xrightarrow{w} s$
ababaa	.00077	.00154	.00154	0.0	.00077	
abaaaa	.00442	.00442	.00442	.00442	.00884	
aaabaa	.00442	.00442	.00442	.00442	.00884	
aaaaaa	.02548	0.0	0.0	.05096	.07644	
Total	.03509	.01038	.01038	.05970	.09489	
Rounded	.035	.01	.01	.06	.095	.165
New $P(\rightarrow)$		.06	1.0	.36	.58	
Next iteration of the training algorithm						
ababaa	.00209	.00418	.00418	0.0	.00209	
abaaaa	.00727	.00727	.00727	.00727	.01454	
aaabaa	.00727	.00727	.00727	.00727	.01454	
aaaaaa	.02529	0.0	0.0	.05058	.07587	
Total	.04192	.01872	.01872	.06512	.10704	
Rounded	.042	.019	.019	.065	.107	.191
New $P(\rightarrow)$		.10	1.0	.34	.56	

Figure 4.10
A training calculation

that can be explained by that transition, and conversely the comparatively low number of outputs that must be explained by the other transition out of state a, cause the counts to be biased slightly in favor of $a \xrightarrow{0} b$ at each iteration of the algorithm.

Unfortunately, there are three limitations on how well this algorithm can do. The least important of these is the fact that in one case the algorithm does not improve the probabilities: if the probabilities are at a *critical point*. Critical points are those places where there is no obvious direction to go in order to make the best improvement. In figure 4.11, point c is a critical point in that there is no way to decide between moving right or moving left: locally they both look equally good. It is like the mule exactly between two bales of hay that starves to death because he cannot decide which one to go to. Saddle points are also critical points.

Nor are such situations just mathematical anomalies. To see how critical points can actually arise, consider the correct and guessed HMMs of figure

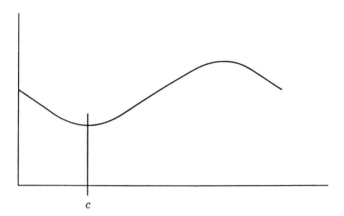

c

Figure 4.11
A critical point

4.12. When we give our training algorithm the incorrect HMM of figure 4.12(b) along with a training sequence "aabb," say, we would like it to learn the HMM in figure 4.12(a), which assigns probability 1/4 to the sequence, rather than the probability 1/16 assigned it by the incorrect version. Unfortunately, the training algorithm cannot improve the initial probabilities. Intuitively, the way to understand this is that somehow the algorithm must decide whether to use state r or s to generate the subsequence "aa." (The subsequence "bb" presents a similar quandary.) As things stand, it is "stuck" in between the two possible assignments, with nothing pushing it one way or the other. More formally, if we apply the algorithm over all possible paths in the incorrect model, we find that they all have the same probability and thus the probability for each of the path sequences stays the same. While this may seem a contrived example (and indeed it is), this sort of thing can actually come up in practice. If it does happen, then adding a little noise to the initial guesses for the probabilities (that is, "randomly" adding or subtracting some small amount to each initial guess) breaks the complete symmetry between the possibilities and enables the training algorithm to assign "roles" to the nodes of the HMM.

A second limitation of our algorithm, this one important, is that the algorithm can never do any better than the training sequence allows. If the training sequence is unrepresentative, then the final probabilities are unrepresentative as well. Note how the probability of $a \xrightarrow{0} a$ in figures 4.9 and 4.10 is decreasing. If we pursued the algorithm to the end we would find that,

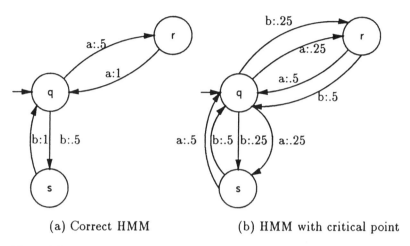

(a) Correct HMM   (b) HMM with critical point

Figure 4.12
An HMM with a critical point

given our training sequence "01011," eventually the probability of a $\overset{0}{\rightarrow}$ a is driven to zero. The reason is simple: the algorithm is trying to make the input as likely as possible. Eventually the "01" sequences are handled by giving a high probability to the path from a to b and back. The "1" at the end causes the probability of a $\overset{1}{\rightarrow}$ a to go to 1/3. But nothing in the input sequence requires a $\overset{0}{\rightarrow}$ a, so the best way to make the input as likely as possible is to make $P(a \overset{0}{\rightarrow} a)$ zero and use the probability mass to make the other transitions out of a higher, and thus the probability of the input higher. Thus the algorithm tends to "over-fit" the parameters to the data unless the training sequence is a good one, or something else is done to prevent it. (We were making a similar point earlier when we noted that the training algorithm would simply memorize the training sequence if it could.)

Finally, and this can often be an important problem, the training algorithm is not guaranteed to find the best probabilities, even in the absence of a critical point. As we have noted, the algorithm adjusts the probabilities to make the training sequence as likely as possible. One way to think of this is to imagine a multidimensional space with one dimension for each transition parameter we are adjusting. At each point in the space there is a corresponding probability that those parameters assign to the training sequence. The training algorithm is a "hill-climbing" scheme to find a point "nearby" the current parameters that assigns higher probability. It continues to do this at each iteration until it reaches a maximum—that is, until it finds a point at which any small change to any combination of the parameters decreases the training probability. At this point the algorithm halts. Unfortunately, the maximum found by the algorithm may be only a *local* maximum: there may be other places in the parameter space that have higher probabilities. In such cases, the initial (guessed) set of parameters determines which (local) maximum the algorithm finds. In chapter 7 we will see problems in which one would like to apply this algorithm (or variations of it) where the number of local maxima is high, and thus one does not, in fact, find the globally best parameters unless one is *very* lucky with the initial guess for the probabilities.

This said, the training algorithm is still very useful. But it needs improvement since the current version, using equation 4.21, requires iterating through all possible paths for the input sequence, which in general grows exponentially with the length of the sequence. We now show how to train in more reasonable time.

Our first step is to transform equation 4.21 into a form that does not count over all possible paths $s_{1,n+1}$:

$$C(s^i \xrightarrow{w^k} s^j) = \frac{1}{P(w_{1,n})} \sum_{t=1}^{n} \sum_{s_{1,n+1}} P(s_{1,n+1}, w_{1,n}) \delta_t(s^i \xrightarrow{w^k} s^j, s_{1,n+1}, w_{1,n}) \quad (4.22)$$

$$= \frac{1}{P(w_{1,n})} \sum_{t=1}^{n} \sum_{s_{1,n+1}} P(S_t = s^i, S_{t+1} = s^j, W_t = w^k, s_{1,n+1}, w_{1,n}) \quad (4.23)$$

Equation 4.22 begins this process. Rather than counting how many times the transition appears in the entire path, equation 4.22 looks to see if the path $s_{1,n+1}$ uses the transition at each time tick t, and sums over all t. We use the $\delta_t(s^i \xrightarrow{w^k} s^j, s_{1,n}, w_{1,n})$ function here, which has value 1 if the transition is used at time t and 0 otherwise. In equation 4.23 we get rid of the delta function by putting the requirement that the path go through the transition directly into the probability we are summing over. That is, by requiring $S_t = s^i$, $S_{t+1} = s^j$, and $W_t = w^k$, we are ensuring that the path goes through the transition from state s^i to state s^j while outputting w^k during time tick t—thus it must go through $s^i \xrightarrow{w^k} s^j$, since otherwise the probability is zero and there is no increment to the count. Now, as a slight modification of equation 3.14 we note that

$$P(w_{1,n}, S_t = s^i, S_{t+1} = s^j, W_t = w^k)$$

$$= \sum_{s_{1,n+1}} P(S_t = s^i, S_{t+1} = s^j, W_t = w^k, s_{1,n+1}, w_{1,n}) \qquad (4.24)$$

This is based upon the fact that the probability is summed over all possible (mutually exclusive) values of $s_{1,n+1}$. When we substitute equation 4.24 into equation 4.23 we get

$$C(s^i \xrightarrow{w^k} s^j) = \frac{1}{P(w_{1,n})} \sum_{t=1}^{n} P(S_t = s^i, S_{t+1} = s^j, W_t = w^k, w_{1,n}) \qquad (4.25)$$

$$= \sum_{t=1}^{n} P(s^i \xrightarrow{s^j} w^k \text{ at time tick } t \mid w_{1,n}) \qquad (4.26)$$

Our future manipulations start from equation 4.25, but we modify it slightly in equation 4.26 to make its import clearer. What equation 4.26 says is that the count for a transition is the sum over all possible time ticks of the probability that the training sequence used that transition at that time tick. This makes sense and, as we have just seen, is equivalent to our original definition in terms of all possible paths.

Now we are in a position to develop a reasonably efficient scheme for finding our estimated counts for HMMs. We start from equation 4.25.

$$C(s^i \xrightarrow{w^k} s^j) = \frac{1}{P(w_{1,n})} \sum_{t=1}^{n} P(S_t = s^i, S_{t+1} = s^j, W_t = w^k, w_{1,n})$$

$$= \frac{1}{P(w_{1,n})} \sum_{t=1}^{n} P(w_{1,t-1}, S_t = s^i, W_t = w^k, S_{t+1} = s^j, w_{t+1,n})$$

$$= \frac{1}{P(w_{1,n})} \sum_{t=1}^{n} P(w_{1,t-1}, S_t = s^i)$$

$$\quad P(W_t = w^k, S_{t+1} = s^j \mid w_{1,t-1}, S_t = s^i)$$

$$\quad P(w_{t+1,n} \mid w_{1,t}, S_t = s^i, S_{t+1} = s^j)$$

$$= \frac{1}{P(w_{1,n})} \sum_{t=1}^{n} P(w_{1,t-1}, S_t = s^i) P(W_t = w^k, S_{t+1} = s^j \mid S_t = s^i)$$

$$\quad P(w_{t+1,n} \mid S_{t+1} = s^j)$$

$$= \frac{1}{P(w_{1,n})} \sum_{t=1}^{n} \alpha_i(t) P(s^i \overset{w^k}{\to} s^j) \beta_j(t+1) \tag{4.27}$$

This last equation is the one we want. We have already seen how to compute the $\alpha_i(t-1)$s and the $\beta_j(t+1)$s efficiently, so to get the counts we simply compute them for all points in our training example and then sum according to equation 4.27.

We can now write the algorithm for the parameter re-estimation program needed to finish off the algorithm of figure 4.8. It is quite simple. We first compute the $\alpha_i(t)$ and $\beta_j(t+1)$ values and then use them in equation 4.27 to get the new counts; these are then used in equation 4.21 to get the new HMM parameter values. Figure 4.13 shows the calculations for the first iteration of training for the HMM of figure 4.9(b). It is useful to compare figure 4.13 against the less efficient scheme illustrated in figure 4.10. Note that the probability assigned to the string based upon the initial probabilities is the same in both calculations, as are the probabilities to be assigned to the transitions for the next round. This is, of course, as it should be. The reader may note that the calculations in figure 4.13 are actually no simpler than those required in figure 4.10 for what we called the less efficient method of calculating the transition counts. This is because the example in figure 4.9 was specifically designed to make the less efficient calculation possible.

4.4 Exercises

4.1 We showed two ways of calculating the probability of a sequence, one using the forward probabilities and taking them to the end of the sequence, the other using backward probabilities and taking them to the start of the sequence. It is also possible to get the probability by combining forward and backward probabilities at any place in the middle of the string. In particular:

$$P(w_{1,n}) = \sum_{i=1}^{\sigma} \alpha_i(t) \beta_i(t) \tag{4.28}$$

Show how this equation reduces to the ones we already have for $t=1$ and $t=n+1$. Prove that this relation is true in general.

4.2 Show in detail that applying our training algorithm to the HMM in figure 4.12 on the training example "aabb" does not change the probabilities assigned to any of the transitions.

	1	2	3	4	5	6
	ϵ	0	1	0	1	1
$\alpha_a(t)$	1	.48	.27	.13	.072	.035
$\alpha_b(t)$	0	.04	0	.01	0	0

	1	2	3	4	5	6
	0	1	0	1	1	ϵ
$\beta_a(t)$	.035	.062	.13	.23	.48	1
$\beta_b(t)$	0	.13	0	.28	1	1

	0	1	0	1	1	Total	New P
$a \xrightarrow{0} b$	.0052	0.0	.0052	0.0	0.0	.010	.06
$b \xrightarrow{1} a$	0.0	.0052	0.0	.0048	0.0	.010	1.0
$a \xrightarrow{0} a$	.030	0.0	.030	0.0	0.0	.060	.36
$a \xrightarrow{1} a$	0.0	.030	0.0	.030	.035	.095	.58

Figure 4.13
Calculations for the first training iteration

4.3 We claimed that our parameter-estimation algorithm computes the probability of our training example (given the current parameters) and thus that this measure could be used to determine when to stop re-estimation. Show that this claim is true.

4.4 Early on in our discussion of HMMs, we noted that we would assume that there were transitions between all possible states for all possible outputs, but that many of these could have zero probability, in which case we could act as if the transition was not there (and we would not show it in the graphical representations of the HMM). It may not be clear that we can get away with this for our training algorithm. For example, can these "pseudo-transitions" be trained to get some non-zero probability? Show that, in fact, this cannot happen; that is, show that a transition with a zero probability always has a zero probability after training with our algorithm.

4.5 In chapter 3 we introduced a part-of-speech tagger in which the language-model transition probabilities were defined to be $P(w_i \mid t_i)\ P(t_{i+1} \mid t_i)$. However, our training mechanism finds the probability of every transition, $P(t_i \xrightarrow{w_i} t_{i+1}) = P(w_i, t_{i+1} \mid t_i)$. Show how to calculate the desired probabilities from those given by the training calculation.

4.6 We can see that some of the numbers in figure 4.13 are the same. In particular:

(a) $\alpha_a(6) = \beta_a(1)$

(b) $\beta_a(6) = \beta_b(6)$

(c) $C(b \xrightarrow{1} a)$ for $t = 2$ is the same as $C(a \xrightarrow{0} b)$ for $t = 3$

(d) $\alpha_a(1) = \beta_a(6)$

(e) $\alpha_a(6) + \alpha_b(6) = \beta_a(1)$

(f) $\alpha_b(1) = \beta_b(1)$

(g) $C(a \xrightarrow{0} b)$ for $t = 2$ is the same as $C(b \xrightarrow{1} a)$ for $t = 3$

For each one, specify which of the following classes it belongs to: (a) it is an invariant in that for any output of this length, and for any HMM with at least two states a and b, this equality would hold (though possibly with different numbers), (b) it is a "semi-invariant" in that for any HMM with the same structure as our HMM but with different probabilities, and for any output of the same length, this equality would hold, but if we changed the structure of the HMM it would not in general hold, or (c) it is a coincidence in that if we changed the probabilities of our HMM in any way, or perhaps just specified more significant digits, this apparent equality would go away. (In all cases, references to time tick 6 should be interpreted as "the last time tick.") Explain your answers.

4.7 Consider a program that finds optimal λs for equation 3.7 by adjusting them so that equation 3.5 assigns as high a probability as possible to a second corpus of English text. This involves implementating a version of the HMM training algorithm, but is simpler than the general case. This is because the data tells us directly how often the HMM reaches the state on the left of figure 3.2. Explain why this is so, and how it simplifies our calculations in the training scheme.

4.8 Implement the program of exercise 4.7. Consider an extension in line with the comments in exercise 3.2. In particular, classify the bigrams $w_{i-2,i-1}$ into three groups, very common bigrams, very rare bigrams, and those in the middle, and then calculate different λs for equation 3.7 for each of these three classes. Modify your program of exercise 3.9 so that it uses the correct λs for each $w_{i-2,i-1}$.

4.9 Implement a program that automatically calculates the parameters for equation 3.30 from an initial guess plus an untagged corpus. Experiment with known corpora (possibly generated by the program of exercise 1.7) to see how well your program performs as a function of the initial guesses for the parameters.

5 Probabilistic Context-Free Grammars

In chapter 1 we pointed out the need for a mechanism (a *syntactic parser*) to find the syntactic structure of a sentence according to some grammar. We looked in particular at context-free grammars (CFGs) and gave some detail on chart parsing.

In this chapter we introduce the notion of a *probabilistic context-free grammar* (PCFG). We look at some of its more basic properties, discuss why one might want a PCFG rather than a regular CFG, and briefly mention some of the more useful algorithms for PCFGs. Actual derivations of the mathematics for these algorithms are given in the next chapter.

5.1 Probabilistic Grammars

A probabilistic context-free grammar is a four-tuple $< W, N, N^1, R >$, where W is a set of terminal symbols $\{w^1, \ldots, w^\omega\}$, N is a set of non-terminal symbols $\{N^1, \ldots N^\nu\}$, N^1 is the starting symbol, and R is a set of rules, each of which is of the form $N^i \rightarrow \zeta^j$, where ζ^j is a string of terminals and non-terminals. (The j is there just in case we wish to distinguish this sequence from other sequences.) Each rule has a probability $P(N^i \rightarrow \zeta^j)$. The probabilities for all the rules that expand the same non-terminal must sum to one. Intuitively, $P(N^i \rightarrow \zeta^j)$ means the probability of expanding the non-terminal N^i using this rule as opposed to any of the other rules for N^i. As with the non-probabilistic version of context-free grammars, we can think of a PCFG as defining a *context-free language* that specifies how to expand the starting symbol into the strings in the language or, conversely, how to assign a structure to a given string in the language. The difference is that a PCFG also assigns a probability to the string such that the probabilities of all the strings sum to one. Figure 5.1 shows a PCFG that generates the sentence "Swat flies like ants." The probability of a sentence in a PCFG is the sum of the probabilities of all possible parses for the sentence. So if $t_{1,n}$ varies over all the possible trees for $w_{1,n}$ then

$$P(w_{1,n}) = \sum_{t_{1,n}} P(w_{1,n}, t_{1,n}) \tag{5.1}$$

$$= \sum_{t_{1,n}} P(t_{1,n}) P(w_{1,n} \mid t_{1,n}) \tag{5.2}$$

$$= \sum_{t_{1,n}} P(t_{1,n}) \tag{5.3}$$

s	→	np vp	: .8	prep	→	like	: 1.0
s	→	vp	: .2	verb	→	swat	: .2
np	→	noun	: .4	verb	→	flies	: .4
np	→	noun pp	: .4	verb	→	like	: .4
np	→	noun np	: .2	noun	→	swat	: .05
vp	→	verb	: .3	noun	→	flies	: .45
vp	→	verb np	: .3	noun	→	ants	: .5
vp	→	verb pp	: .2				
vp	→	verb np pp	: .2				
pp	→	prep np	: 1.0				

Figure 5.1
A PCFG

(The last line here follows because the tree includes the terminals, so the probability of the words given the tree is 1.0.)

There are several possible readings for "Swat flies like ants" given the grammar of figure 5.1. The most intuitive is as a command to swat flies. Figure 5.2 shows one of the less intuitive ones, which says that a certain kind of fly called a "swat fly" happens to like ants. The probability of each parse is the product of the probabilities of all of the rules used in the parse tree. The probability of the parse in figure 5.2 is $.8 \times .2 \times .4 \times .05 \times .45 \times .3 \times .4 \times .4 \times .5 = 3.5 \cdot 10^{-5}$. Note that the probability of a rule used more than once in a parse appears in the product that same number of times; in the parse of figure 5.2 the rule np → noun is used twice, so its probability, .4, is multiplied in twice to arrive at $3.5 \cdot 10^{-5}$.

As with Markov models, we can derive the product rule for tree probabilities given certain assumptions about subtree independence. To see how this works we need a new definition and a new piece of notation. In a parse tree corresponding to a derivation D, we say that a non-terminal N *dominates* constituents $t_{i,j}$ if in D all of $t_{i,j}$ are derived (directly or indirectly) from N. If a non-terminal N^j dominates the terminal string starting at k and ending at l, we write $N^j_{k,l}$. This is shown in figure 5.3. Using this notation, we can now more formally define what we mean by the probability of a tree and the probability of a rule. First, the probability of a tree is the probability that all of its constituents dominate the correct parts of the terminal string, given

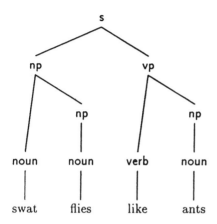

Figure 5.2
A parse of "Swat flies like ants"

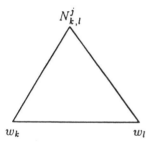

Figure 5.3
A non-terminal starting at k and ending at l

that the start symbol dominates the entire terminal string. Consider the tree in figure 5.4. Assuming that A is the start symbol, its probability is given by:

$$P(\text{figure 5.4}) = P(A_{1,5}, B_{1,3}, C_{4,5}, w_1, w_2, w_3, w_4, w_5 \mid A_{1,5}) \tag{5.4}$$

The probability of a rule is as follows:

$$P(N^j \rightarrow XY \ldots Z) \stackrel{\text{def}}{=} P(X_{k,m}, Y_{m+1,n}, \ldots, Z_{q+1,l} \mid N^j_{k,l}) \tag{5.5}$$

This is to say that the probability of a rule is the probability that the constituents on the right-hand side of the rule dominate a string $w_{k,l}$ given that the constituent on the left-hand side of the rule dominates that string of words.

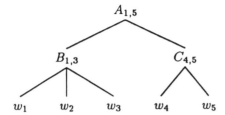

Figure 5.4
A tree to illustrate the product rule for tree probabilities

This equality is true for any k and l and any m, n, ..., p, q provided that $k \leq m \leq n \ldots \leq p \leq q \leq l$.

While we are, of course, free to define our rule probabilities any way we choose, one aspect of this rule could seem unreasonable. Suppose that in the above rule X is a non-terminal for some structure that always requires at least three words to complete. In this case, is it reasonable to say that the probability of the rule when X dominates a string of length 1 is the same as the probability of the rule when X dominates a string of length 3 or greater? It turns out that, yes, this is reasonable. The reason is that the length of X comes out in terms like $P(w_k \mid X_{k,k})$, which in this case is zero.

Now we state (somewhat informally) our independence assumption for PCFGs:

$$P(N_{k,l}^j \to \zeta^m \mid \text{anything outside of } k \text{ through } l) = P(N_{k,l}^j \to \zeta^m) \qquad (5.6)$$

$$P(N_{k,l}^j \to \zeta^m \mid \text{anything above } N_{k,l}^j \text{ in the tree}) = P(N_{k,l}^j \to \zeta^m) \qquad (5.7)$$

Finally, given these more formal definitions of the probabilities of trees and rules and given the independence assumptions, we can show that the probability of a particular parse tree is the product of the rules that made it up. Consider again the tree in figure 5.4. The probability for this tree structure can be computed as follows:

$$
\begin{aligned}
P(\text{figure 5.4}) &= P(A_{1,5}, B_{1,3}, C_{4,5}, w_1, w_2, w_3, w_4, w_5 \mid A_{1,5}) \\
&= P(B_{1,3}, C_{4,5} \mid A_{1,5})P(w_1, w_2, w_3 \mid A_{1,5}, B_{1,3}, C_{4,5}) \\
&\quad P(w_4, w_5 \mid A_{1,5}, B_{1,3}, C_{4,5}, w_{1,3}) \\
&= P(B_{1,3}, C_{4,5} \mid A_{1,5})P(w_1, w_2, w_3 \mid B_{1,3})P(w_4, w_5 \mid C_{4,5}) \\
&= P(A \to BC)P(B \to w_1 w_2 w_3)P(C \to w_4 w_5)
\end{aligned}
$$

The first line is just the definition of the probability of the tree. The second conditionalizes it to get the terms we want. The third line applies the independence assumptions for PCFGs, and the final line just substitutes in for the definitions of the probabilities of the PCFG rules.

5.2   PCFGs and Syntactic Ambiguity

PCFGs are sufficiently like CFGs that the reader by now should have a basic idea of how they work. What might not be so obvious is why one would want a PCFG anyway. Traditionally one wants a grammar for a language because it assigns a structure to a sentence, and typically one wants this structure because it gives a guide to the meaning of the sentence. Since any structure that could be assigned by a PCFG could be assigned by a CFG, why introduce probabilities? In this and the following three sections we provide some answers.

Perhaps the most obvious advantage of a PCFG comes in cases of syntactic ambiguity. When a sentence has more than one parse one would like to know which parse was intended. PCFGs give an ordering of the parses by assigning each one a probability. Consider again our example "Swat flies like ants." Figure 5.2 gives a less intuitive parse for this sentence, one that is assigned a probability of $3.5 \cdot 10^{-5}$; figure 5.5 gives its most intuitive parse, the probability of which, according to the grammar in figure 5.1, is $2.88 \cdot 10^{-4}$. Thus in this case, at least, the grammar assigns the higher probability to the more intuitive parse.

Despite the happy result in the last paragraph, by itself a PCFG's ability to order parses correctly is not all that great. (In particular, see exercise 5.1.) All the PCFG can do in this regard is to prefer more common constructions of the language over less common ones. While this is often important, the particular words of the sentence can be at least as important in deciding the correct syntactic interpretation. For example, consider the prepositional-phrase-attachment ambiguity illustrated by these two sentences:

Alice bought a plant with Mary.

Alice bought a plant with yellow leaves.

Statistically, prepositional phrases attach to noun phrases ("a plant with yellow leaves") slightly more often than to verb phrases ("bought something

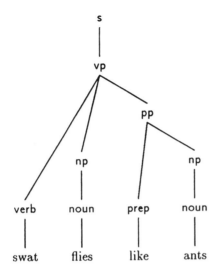

Figure 5.5
The intuitive parse of "Swat flies like ants"

with Mary"). However, the difference is small and the real deciding factor
is the particular words in question (and presumably their meaning). This is a
topic to which we return in chapter 8. As we show there, PCFGs in conjunction with other mechanisms do help with this problem. Our point here is that
on their own PCFGs probably are not very useful in syntactic disambiguation.

5.3   PCFGs and Grammar Induction

One less obvious advantage of PCFGs over CFGs is in grammar learning.
At first glance, CFGs might seem preferable in this endeavor, since learning
a PCFG forces one to learn the CFG *plus* the probabilities associated with
the rules. There are other considerations, however, that offset this additional
burden. To make our point we need to digress briefly to discuss some basic
issues in grammar learning, or *grammar induction* as it is usually called.

An important distinction in grammar induction is that between *positive
training examples* and *negative training examples*. A positive training example
is a sentence (or some other kind of string) that is in the language defined
by the grammar. In our statistical work these examples are provided by a
corpus. Negative training examples are examples of strings that are not in

the language. For instance, "in distinction important an," the first four words of this paragraph in reverse order, is generally not considered a grammatical string of English. Unfortunately, it is now known that it is not possible to learn a context-free language unless one has *both* positive and negative training examples.

Actually, the problem of grammar induction is more severe than this and one in fact needs several kinds of *oracles*. An oracle is a device that answers questions correctly. One oracle needed for grammar induction answers, for any string, "Is this string in the language?" Another necessary oracle takes a grammar and, if it is not the correct one, responds with a string that is a counterexample to the grammar. For a general survey of non-probabilistic grammar induction, see [2,3,21]. However, this is not of concern to us here.

It is not to hard to see why negative examples are so important in CFG learning. Let us again make the common assumption that English has a fixed number of words $w^1, \ldots, w^\omega$. Consider the "grammar" of English shown in figure 5.6. If we have only positive training examples there is nothing obviously wrong with it. After all, it generates all of the positive examples in our corpus. The problem is that it would generate all possible negative examples as well, but without such examples there is no way to know this.

The necessity of negative examples is problematic for our statistical approach, as we have been tacitly assuming that all the corpora at our disposal are positive examples—and a good assumption this is! But it is not just statistical language processing that must worry about negative examples. There is evidence that children learn the grammar of their native language without such examples either. In particular, parents rarely correct children's grammar. Thus cognitive psychologists have the problem of accounting for children's ability to learn their language in the face of the lack of such apparently necessary correction.

Probabilistic grammars may offer a way out of this problem. Consider again the simple grammar of figure 5.6, but now viewed as a PCFG with all non-zero probabilities. This still generates all of the sentences in our corpus, but the probability it assigns them is presumably quite low compared to what a correct grammar for English might assign. After all, the grammar of figure 5.6 assigns non-zero probabilities to a lot of sentences that never appear in our corpus. Indeed, since the most common word in English is "the," the most common sentence in English according to the grammar of figure 5.6 might well be "the." The probability that this grammar assigns to such negative examples must be taken away from those of the correct examples. Thus a

s	$\rightarrow$	word s
s	$\rightarrow$	word
word	$\rightarrow$	w^1
word	$\rightarrow$	w^2
	$\cdots$	
word	$\rightarrow$	w^ω

Figure 5.6
A trivial grammar for English

search for a PCFG that assigned our corpus as high a probability as possible would presumably reject this grammar, despite the fact that it covers all of the positive examples. Thus it may be the case that learning PCFGs does not require the negative examples required for CFGs. At any rate, the simple examples that show the limitations of positive training examples for regular CFG induction do not argue against the probabilistic case.

5.4 PCFGs and Ungrammaticality

Another advantage of PCFGs over CFGs is in the area of ungrammatical sentences. A common objection to grammars in general is that corpora frequently contain ungrammatical structures that a standard grammar would reject. One solution is simply to include rules that generate *all* of the things one sees in English text, grammatical or not. An objection to this approach is that such a grammar would fail to distinguish between anomalous strings that happen to occur from time to time and those that are truly part of the language. Furthermore, it is argued, such a move would have profound effects on grammar induction. Almost any string *might* occur in a corpus. Thus the simple grammar of figure 5.6 might be the "correct" one after all!

Again, PCFGs offer a possible way out of this problem. Imagine, for example, a grammar that has two parts. The first, our "normal" grammar, assigns probabilities to sentences we normally think of as grammatical. Presumably these probabilities would be relatively high, as most of the sentences we encounter are indeed grammatical. The second part would be something like figure 5.6. It would assign probabilities to the ungrammatical cases, which would be much lower. One could imagine an even more complicated PCFG to handle sentences that were mostly grammatical but had bad patches. This would use the normal rules whenever possible but invoke the trivial grammar to paper over the bad parts.

We would not want to claim that this solves the ungrammatical-sentence problem. For example, it says nothing about why some kinds of ungrammaticality are more common than others. However, our purpose here is not to solve these thorny problems, but rather simply to note that PCFGs give one an extra degree of freedom when approaching them.

There is, however, one aspect of our discussion of ungrammaticality to which we must commit ourselves. If we are going to build language models using PCFGs (and we argue shortly that this is a good idea), then the PCFG cannot afford to assign a zero probability to any string, no matter how ungrammatical, for fear that this string might occur in a corpus. Book this in found be can ungrammaticality! Thus in our discussion we assume that our grammars are permissive in that they rule out nothing.

5.5 PCFGs and Language Modeling

The last of our reasons for studying PCFGs has to do with language modeling. A PCFG for English would immediately give us a language model for English, as any string of English is simply a sequence of sentences and the probability of the whole would simply be the product of the probabilities of the individual sentences. However, this turns out not to produce a very good language model—the trigram model of chapter 3 does better!

That the trigram model does better might at first seem strange. After all, this model assigns non-zero probabilities to many ungrammatical sentences of English, and by our earlier argument, this must mean that it assigns a lower probability to the grammatical ones than it could do otherwise. However, our PCFG has its own drawbacks as a language model. To understand them, consider how such a model would surely work. Look again at the grammar of figure 5.1. It can be thought of as having two basic kinds of rules. Those in the first column are the "true" grammar rules, while those in the second column are *lexical rules*—rules that define the lexicon of the language. Furthermore, note how this grammar produces a sentence. First the grammatical rules of the language produce a string of parts of speech and then the lexical rules substitute words for them. It is in this second phase that the loss of probability is most acute. The problem is that our grammars are, by definition, context-free. Consider a noun phrase like "the green banana."

A trigram model of English would presumably assign a relatively high probability to "banana" given that it comes after the words "the green." Our PCFG would probably do much less well on the probability it assigned to "banana," as it is not a very common noun. Remember, the rule n → banana, which substituted "banana" into our sentence, has no knowledge of the context in which this substitution is taking place—this is, after all, why context-free grammars are called "context-free." Thus many more common nouns, like "time," "number," "year," etc., would all be assigned higher probability by our PCFG than would "banana," despite the fact that given the context the latter is surely a more likely choice. Thus the trigram model can do better because it has at least *some* ability to take context into account, while the PCFG has none.

So simply using a PCFG as a language model is not a good idea. Nevertheless, there are good reasons to believe that a language model using PCFGs in conjunction with knowledge of lexical context could do better than the trigram model. Consider a sentence like

Fred watered his mother's small garden.

In particular, consider the contribution to the probability from the word "garden." A trigram model would not do particularly well here, since the probability

$$P(\text{garden} \mid \text{mother's small}) \tag{5.8}$$

is presumably not all that high. On the other hand, suppose we had parsed the sentence and knew that "his mother's small garden" was the direct object of the verb "to water." Now consider this probability:

$$P(X = \text{garden} \mid X \text{ is head of direct object noun phrase of "to water"}) \quad (5.9)$$

(Here we have used the notion of a *head constituent* in a phrase. Intuitively, this is the most important or defining constituent of that phrase: the noun in a noun phrase, verb in a verb phrase, or preposition in a prepositional phrase.) The probability of equation 5.9 would be much higher than that of equation 5.8, as watering gardens is quite common. Here we have considered a very simple model in which the probability of a word is conditioned only on the role it plays in the next higher constituent, and the head of that constituent. That is, the constituent above the noun phrase in question is the verb phrase the head of which is "water."

Another benefit of such a model is that it would have, if anything, fewer parameters than a trigram model. As we have already noted, a trigram model must consider all possible combinations of three English words. The model we sketch here needs only pairs of words and the syntactic relation between them. As there are presumably fewer syntactic relations than words, the model has fewer parameters.

It should be clear, however, that a standard CFG will not do here. To make this more concrete, consider the basics of the language model we are talking about. The probability of the corpus is the product of the probabilities of the sentences, and the probability of a sentence is the sum of the probability of all of its possible parses. However, this model uses the PCFG only to predict the parts of speech and the syntactic relations among them. It does not get down to the level of lexical items since, as we have already argued, PCFGs are not very good at predicting the actual words. Thus we get the following expression, where t_j is the jth parse of the sentence:

$$P(s) = \sum_j P(t_j)P(s \mid t_j) \tag{5.10}$$

(Note that if we considered the parse as specifying the sequence of words then $P(s \mid t_j)$ would always be one.) Here the term $P(t_j)$ is the probability of the parse. A PCFG would, of course, give us this quantity, while a regular CFG would not. This is the basis of our claim that PCFGs could be used to construct better language models. In chapter 8 we consider this model in more detail.

5.6 Basic Algorithms for PCFGs

The next chapter is devoted to deriving the mathematics behind the standard algorithms of PCFGs. In essence they parallel those for HMMs. First there are efficient algorithms for finding the probability of a string. As we have noted, the probability of a string according to a PCFG is simply the sum of the probability of its parses. Unfortunately, as pointed out in chapter 1, the number of parses for a sentence can grow exponentially in the length of the sentence, so simply summing over them is not efficient enough. There is also an algorithm for finding the most probable parse according to a PCFG. This is similar to the algorithm for finding the most probable path through an HMM that would produce a given string.

Perhaps most important, there is a training algorithm for PCFG probabilities. As with HMM training, the algorithm takes a PCFG and a corpus and adjusts the probabilities on the PCFG rules so the grammar assigns a higher probability to the corpus. It is also similar to HMM training in its limitations—the algorithm is guaranteed only to find a local maximum.

5.7 Exercises

5.1 In figure 5.5 we gave the parse tree for the most intuitive reading of "Swat flies like ants." We also found that the probability of this parse was higher than that of the parse in figure 5.2. Unfortunately, this is not the parse to which the grammar of figure 5.1 assigns the highest probability. Find this other parse and its probability.

5.2 In section 5.5 we presented a simple language model based upon PCFGs and the lexical relations among the heads of various constituents. Give an informal argument that such a model ought to do as well as the trigram model on "the green banana," the example we used to argue against PCFGs used alone.

6 The Mathematics of PCFGs

In this chapter we derive the mathematics for two of the major algorithms for PCFGs. First we consider how to find the probability assigned to a string by a PCFG. We also show how the chart-parsing algorithm of chapter 1, slightly modified, can perform this task. We then look at the training algorithm for PCFGs. In both algorithms the mathematics closely resembles that for HMMs, so we start by looking at the relation between the two.

6.1 Relation of HMMs to PCFGs

While PCFGs look quite different from our previous probabilistic mechanism, the HMM, it turns out there are remarkable similarities. The best way to see this is to consider a simpler kind of grammar called a *probabilistic regular grammar*. A probabilistic regular grammar is just a PCFG in which the rules are restricted to be of the forms $N^i \rightarrow w^j N^k$ or $N^i \rightarrow w^j$. A *regular language* is a language generated by a regular grammar. For example, here are the rules for a regular grammar that can generate any string of 0s and 1s, but assigns higher probability to strings made up of groups of two symbols in which the first symbol is 0:

$$
\begin{array}{|lll|lll|lll|}
s & \rightarrow & 0\ b : .9 & s & \rightarrow & 1\ s : .05 & s & \rightarrow & 0\ s : .05 \\
b & \rightarrow & 1\ s : .3 & b & \rightarrow & 1 : .1 & b & \rightarrow & 0\ s : .5 \\
b & \rightarrow & 0 : .1 & & & & & &
\end{array}
$$

Here s is the start symbol.

Now consider the HMM in figure 6.1. Here we have made each non-terminal of our grammar into a state of the HMM and made each rule of the form $N^i \rightarrow w^j N^k$ into the HMM transition $N^i \xrightarrow{w^j} N^k$. Furthermore, when we consider a parse of a string according to the grammar (for example, figure 6.2 gives two parse trees for "0001"), we can see that each sequence of states of the HMM that would generate the string corresponds to the sequence of non-terminals in a possible parse tree.

Note, however, that there is nothing in an HMM that corresponds to a regular grammar rule of the form $N^i \rightarrow w^j$. This is because the two concepts, probabilistic regular grammars and HMMs, are not exactly the same. The difference is in the way they assign probabilities. A probabilistic grammar assigns a probability to each string of a language such that the probability of all strings sums to one. (We often use the word "sentence" to describe such a string.) Thus each sentence of the language is considered a random event.

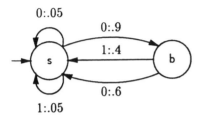

Figure 6.1
An HMM similar to the sample regular grammar

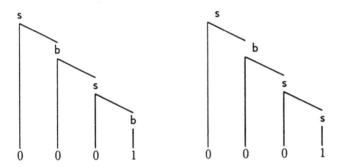

Figure 6.2
Two parse trees of a regular grammar output

With HMMs we consider sequences of a particular length n, and then the probability of all possible sequences of length n sums to one.

To make this distinction more dramatic, consider the probability each model might assign to the string "Alice went to the." An HMM for a bit of English would assign it a relatively high probability. In particular, it would be *higher* than the probability for, say, "Alice went to the office," since the latter would require another transition whose probability would most likely be less than one. On the other hand, a grammar for English would assign the complete sentence a relatively high probability and the incomplete one a much lower probability.

So the two notions are clearly different. Nevertheless, the similarities are great, and many of the concepts developed for HMM have direct correlates needed in our analysis of PCFGs.

6.2   Finding Sentence Probabilities for PCFGs

In this section we consider how to determine the probability of a sentence according to a PCFG. However, we restrict our proofs to the case when the CFG is in Chomksy-normal form (CNF). The reader may remember CNF as one of the restricted CFGs mentioned in chapter 1. In CNF all rules are of the forms $N^i \rightarrow w^j$ or $N^i \rightarrow N^j N^k$. In the rest of this chapter we formally derive our mechanisms only for the case that the grammar has this restrictive form. The proofs, however, are in fact quite general, and after we have derived the equations for the Chomsky-normal case we present the final equations for the more general case as well. It should not be too hard to see how the general case follows from the proofs for the restricted case, but creating the notation for proving the general case can get tedious and we omit it here.

In deriving the probability of a sentence it is useful to keep in mind the analogy between HMMs and regular grammars. In particular, consider the forward and backward probabilities, $\alpha_i(t)$ and $\beta_i(t)$, used in chapter 4 as alternative ways of finding the probability of a given word sequence. We repeat here the definitions in equations 4.8 and 4.13:

$$\alpha_i(t) \stackrel{\text{def}}{=} P(w_{1,t-1}, S_t = s^i)$$

$$\beta_i(t) \stackrel{\text{def}}{=} P(w_{t,n} \mid S_t = s^i)$$

First consider $\beta_i(t)$. Looking at the trees of figure 6.2 as sequences of HMM states leads to the observation that $\beta_i(t)$ can be thought of as the probability that the non-terminal N^i expands into the sequence $w_{t,n}$. Or, to put it slightly differently, $\beta_i(t)$ is the probability of getting the sequence $w_{t,n}$ given that the non-terminal N^i spans that sequence in the parse tree. Because of the simple structure of the trees generated by regular grammars, it is possible to denote the words dominated by a non-terminal using a single number, t. As implicitly noted in figure 5.3, indicating the portion of the terminal string dominated by a non-terminal in a context-free parse requires two numbers. We have chosen to use the number of the first and last terminals in the string (typically k and l). Thus the backward probability gets converted to this:

$$\beta_j(k, l) \stackrel{\text{def}}{=} P(w_{k,l} \mid N^j_{k,l}) \tag{6.1}$$

We call $\beta_j(k, l)$ the *inside probability* as it denotes the probability of the terminals "inside" $N^j_{k,l}$.

What we previously called the forward probability $\alpha_i(t)$ can be recast in a context-free light as well. Again looking at figure 6.2, we can see that the forward probability for the non-terminal N^i at the position in the tree defined by t is the probability of producing the material before (or "outside") N^i while N^i dominates the rest of the material. Figure 6.3 shows this situation for a context-free parse tree. With this in mind we define the *outside probability* as:

$$\alpha_j(k,l) \stackrel{\text{def}}{=} P(w_{1,k-1}, N^j_{k,l}, w_{l+1,n}) \tag{6.2}$$

We can now use both the inside and the outside probabilities to derive the probability of a sentence according to a PCFG. We start with the inside probability method. Once we have the inside probabilities we can get the probability of the sentence as follows:

$$\beta_1(1,n) = P(w_{1,n} \mid N^1_{1,n})$$
$$= P(w_{1,n})$$

Next we show how to calculate the inside probabilities efficiently. We start with the base case, computing $\beta_j(k,k)$. In Chomsky-normal form there is only one possible way that the non-terminal N^j can dominate the material w_k, and that is if there is a rule $N^j \rightarrow w_k$. Thus we have:

$$\beta_j(k,k) = P(w_k \mid N^j_{k,k})$$
$$= P(N^j \rightarrow w_k) \tag{6.3}$$

Next consider the case when $l > k$. Here we consider all possible ways that the material dominated by $N^j_{k,l}$ can be derived. At the topmost level there must be some rule with N^j on the left-hand side, and since we have restricted ourselves to Chomsky-normal form the rule must be of the form $N^j \rightarrow N^p N^q$. This situation is shown in more detail in figure 6.4. Note that we also introduce a new variable m that is the last terminal in the material dominated by N^p. This can vary between k and $l-1$ depending on how N^p and N^q divide up $w_{k,l}$. Thus, to find all possible ways that N^j could be built up out of smaller components, we consider all possible combinations of p, q, and m.

$$\beta_j(k,l) \stackrel{\text{def}}{=} P(w_{k,l} \mid N^j_{k,l})$$
$$= \sum_{p,q,m} P(w_{k,m}, N^p_{k,m}, w_{m+1,l}, N^q_{m+1,l} \mid N^j_{k,l})$$

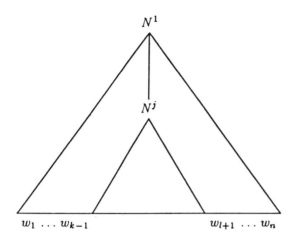

Figure 6.3
The words "outside of" a context-free non-terminal

$$= \sum_{p,q,m} P(N^p_{k,m}, N^q_{m+1,l} \mid N^j_{k,l}) P(w_{k,m} \mid N^j_{k,l}, N^p_{k,m}, N^q_{m+1,l})$$

$$P(w_{m+1,l} \mid w_{k,m}, N^j_{k,l}, N^p_{k,m}, N^q_{m+1,l})$$

$$= \sum_{p,q,m} P(N^p_{k,m}, N^q_{m+1,l} \mid N^j_{k,l}) P(w_{k,m} \mid N^p_{k,m}) P(w_{m+1,l} \mid N^q_{m+1,l}) \qquad (6.98)$$

$$= \sum_{p,q,m} P(N^j \rightarrow N^p N^q) \beta_p(k,m) \beta_q(m+1,l) \qquad (6.99)$$

Here we take the definition and first break it into all possible ways in which the probability can occur and sum over them. We then conditionalize to get the terms we need. In equation 6.4 we use the context-free version of the Markov assumption from equations 5.6 and 5.7. Equation 6.5 is simply a substitution of definitions. It is this last equation that we want, of course, because it tells us how to compute the inside probability from the inside probabilities of smaller constituents. This plus equation 6.3 enables us to build up the inside probabilities starting with constituents of length one and working up to the entire sentence.

Now let us consider how this generalizes for grammars that are not in Chomsky-normal form. Our discussion in chapter 1 of finding parse trees from a chart pointed out that we need to track how the larger constituents of the chart were built up out of the smaller ones, and we saw how to do

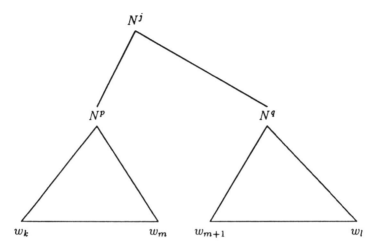

Figure 6.4
How material under $N_{k,l}^j$ could be derived

this by recording on each chart entry the set of completed edges that could be used to build up that constituent at that place in the chart (for the given sentence). We used the notation $\mathcal{E}_{k,l}^j$ to denote the set of edges used to create the chart entry $N_{k,l}^j$. Now given this set, in the derivation of equation 6.5 we could find $\beta_j(k,l)$ by summing over the members of the $\mathcal{E}_{k,l}^j$ rather than over p, q, and m. In what follows we assume that a completed edge $e \in \mathcal{E}_{k,l}^j$ has the following functions associated with it:

$\text{rule}(e) = $ the rule $N^j \to \zeta^i$ used for the edge

$\text{rhs}(e) = $ the sequence of chart entries used

$\text{lhs}(e) = j$

$\text{start}(e) = k$

$\text{end}(e) = l$

Now look again at the main equation above, equation 6.5. As already noted, the sum over p, q, and m is equivalent to summing over all the possible completed edges $e \in \mathcal{E}_{k,l}^j$. The other thing to note is that the term $\beta_p(k,m)$ $\beta_q(m+1,l)$ on the right-hand side of the equation is just the product of the inside probabilities of the constituents that built up the edge. With this in mind we get the general equation for inside probabilities:

$$\beta_j(k,l) = \sum_{e \in \mathcal{E}^j_{k,l}} P(\text{rule}(e)) \prod_{X^m_{n,o} \in \text{rhs}(e)} \beta_m(n,o) \tag{6.6}$$

Note that on the right-hand side of general PCFG rules there can be both terminal and non-terminal symbols. This is why we introduced the symbol $X^m_{n,o}$ in equation 6.6: it can denote either the non-terminal chart entry $N^m_{n,o}$ or a terminal symbol $W_n = w^m$. In the former case we have already defined the inside probability. In the latter case we need to generalize the notion slightly. Since the inside probability is the probability of the terminal string given a dominating non-terminal, then obviously the probability of a terminal character given a terminal character is 1. Thus, if $X^m_{n,o}$ denotes w^m we have

$$\beta_m(n,n) = P(W_n = w^m \mid W_n = w^m) = 1.0 \tag{6.7}$$

Equation 6.7 also serves as the new base case for the recursion, replacing equation 6.3.

Later it will be useful to have the inside probability of an edge, defined as:

$$\beta(e) \stackrel{\text{def}}{=} P(\text{rule}(e)) \prod_{X^m_{n,o} \in \text{rhs}(e)} \beta_m(n,o) \tag{6.8}$$

With this definition we can restate equation 6.6 as:

$$\beta_j(k,l) = \sum_{e \in \mathcal{E}^j_{k,l}} \beta(e) \tag{6.9}$$

To put equation 6.9 in words, the probability of a non-terminal is the sum of the probabilities of all the ways in which that non-terminal could be created.

To see how this works, let us calculate the probability of "Swat flies like ants" according to our example grammar of figure 5.1. Figure 6.5 shows the chart for the parse; however, rather than simply showing the chart entries, we also show the completed edges. For example, in chart position (2, 3) we both show that there is an np and a vp starting at word 2 and having length 3, and also indicate the edge that built each up (or at least we have put in the rule that the edge used). We also indicate the inside probability for each edge. We have felt free, however, to omit any chart entry (and associated edge) that does not figure in a complete parse of the sentence. Note in particular that we have two edges for chart entry (1, 4), both using the rule s → np vp. This

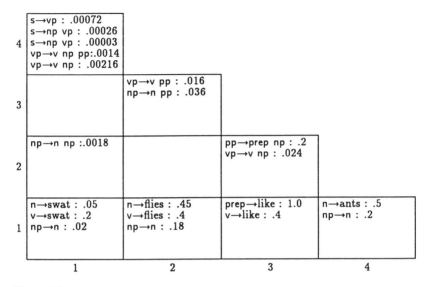

Figure 6.5
Chart and inside edge probabilities for "Swat flies like ants"

is because there are two edges that use this rule to build up an s, but they combine different sub-constituents to do so.

Finally, we can determine the probability of a sentence according to a PCFG using outside probabilities. As in our discussion of HMMs, we develop both methods of determining the probability of a sentence because we need the quantities used therein for our training algorithm. Again we do the proof assuming that all rules are in Chomsky-normal form and then show how to generalize the equation. To see how to calculate the probability of the sentence from the outside probabilities, consider:

$$
\begin{aligned}
P(w_{1,n}) &= \sum_j P(w_{1,k-1}, w_k, w_{k+1,n}, N_{k,k}^j) \\
&= \sum_j P(w_{1,k-1}, N_{k,k}^j, w_{k+1,n}) P(w_k \mid w_{1,k-1}, N_{k,k}^j, w_{k+1,n}) \\
&= \sum_j \alpha_j(k,k) P(N^j \rightarrow w_k) \qquad (6.104)
\end{aligned}
$$

Equation 6.10 works for any k, so we can simply choose a word w_k and use it to calculate $P(w_{1,n})$.

Now we need to show how to calculate the outside probabilities efficiently. Outside probabilities are calculated from the top of the tree working down. Thus the base case is the outside probability for the start state with nothing on the outside:

$$\alpha_1(1,n) = P(N^1_{1,n}) = 1.0 \tag{6.11}$$

That is, we know with certainty that a sentence in the language has the starting symbol dominating the entire sentence.

Next, suppose we want to calculate the outside probability for $N^j_{k,l}$. As we want to do this from the outside probabilities for larger constituents, consider how this constituent could have arisen from higher constituents. Since the rules are in Chomsky-normal form, there are the two possibilities shown in figure 6.6, arising from rules of the form $N^p \rightarrow N^q N^j$ and $N^p \rightarrow N^j N^q$. To find the outside probability $\alpha_j(k,l)$ we sum the outside probabilities over all possible ways in which $N^j_{k,l}$ could arise, and thus we get two terms, one for each of the two possibilities in figure 6.6. In the second term we restrict $q \neq j$ to avoid counting the possible rule $N^p \rightarrow N^j N^j$ twice.

$$
\begin{aligned}
\alpha_j(k,l) &\stackrel{\text{def}}{=} P(w_{1,k-1}, N^j_{k,l}, w_{l+1,n}) \\
&= \sum_{h,p,q} P(w_{1,h-1}, w_{h,k-1}, N^j_{k,l}, w_{l+1,n}, N^p_{h,l}, N^q_{h,k-1}) \\
&\quad + \sum_{m,p,q \neq j} P(w_{1,k-1}, N^j_{k,l}, w_{l+1,m}, w_{m+1,n}, N^p_{k,m}, N^q_{l+1,m}) \\
&= \sum_{h,p,q} P(w_{1,h-1}, N^p_{h,l}, w_{l+1,n}) \\
&\qquad P(N^q_{h,k-1}, N^j_{k,l} \mid w_{1,h-1}, N^p_{h,l}, w_{l+1,n}) \\
&\qquad P(w_{h,k-1} \mid N^q_{h,k-1}, N^j_{k,l}, w_{1,h-1}, N^p_{h,l}, w_{l+1,n}) \\
&\quad + \sum_{m,p,q \neq j} P(w_{1,k-1}, N^p_{k,m}, w_{m+1,n}) \\
&\qquad P(N^j_{k,l}, N^q_{l+1,m} \mid w_{1,k-1}, N^p_{k,m}, w_{m+1,n}) \\
&\qquad P(w_{l+1,m} \mid N^q_{l+1,m}, N^j_{k,l}, w_{1,k-1}, N^p_{k,m}, w_{m+1,n}) \\
&= \sum_{h,p,q} P(w_{1,h-1}, N^p_{h,l}, w_{l+1,n}) P(N^q_{h,k-1}, N^j_{k,l} \mid N^p_{h,l}) P(w_{h,k-1} \mid N^q_{h,k-1}) \\
&\quad + \sum_{m,p,q \neq j} P(w_{1,k-1}, N^p_{k,m}, w_{m+1,n}) P(N^j_{k,l}, N^q_{l+1,m} \mid N^p_{k,m}) \\
&\qquad P(w_{l+1,m} \mid N^q_{l+1,m})
\end{aligned}
$$

$$= \sum_{h,p,q} \alpha_p(h,l)P(N^p{\rightarrow}N^qN^j)\beta_q(h,k-1)$$

$$+ \sum_{m,p,q} \alpha_p(k,m)P(N^p{\rightarrow}N^jN^q)\beta_q(l+1,m) \tag{6.12}$$

And again, just as in the recursive calculation of the inside probabilities, we can generalize our calculation for outside probabilities to arbitrary context-free rules. We can replace the sums over p, q, h, and m in equation 6.12 by a sum over all of the completed edges in which $N^j_{k,l}$ appears, i.e., $\bar{\mathcal{E}}^j_{k,l}$. Just rephrasing equation 6.12 in this way gives us:

$$\alpha_j(k,l) = \sum_{e \in \bar{\mathcal{E}}^j_{k,l}} \alpha_{\text{lhs}(e)}(\text{start}(e), \text{end}(e))P(\text{rule}(e))\beta_q(r,s) \tag{6.13}$$

Here r and s are defined by $N^q_{r,s} \in \text{rhs}(e)$ and $N^q_{r,s} \neq N^j_{k,l}$. That is, the last term in equation 6.13 is the inside probability of the chart entry in the edge other than the one for which we are computing the outside probability. Note that when we express things this way we do not need the two separate sums for the two different ways that $N^j_{k,l}$ could be part of higher rules.

We can also rewrite equation 6.13 using the outside probability of edges:

$$\alpha_j(k,l) = \sum_{e \in \bar{\mathcal{E}}^j_{k,l}} \alpha_{\text{lhs}(e)}(\text{start}(e), \text{end}(e))\frac{\beta(e)}{\beta_j(k,l)} \tag{6.14}$$

This is, in fact, the general equation we want since it does not assume anything about the form of the context-free rule used in making the edge. In figure 6.7 we show the outside probabilities for "Swat flies like ants." Note that here we give the outside probabilities for the chart entries, not the edges as in figure 6.5. This is because the equation for computing outside probabilities itself requires the outside probability of higher chart entries, and also, as we show in the next section, the equations for training a PCFG use this term as well.

6.3 Training PCFGs

In this section we develop the algorithm for training the probabilities of a PCFG. As in our HMM training, the algorithm starts with a training corpus and some initial guess at the probabilities, and adjusts the probabilities to

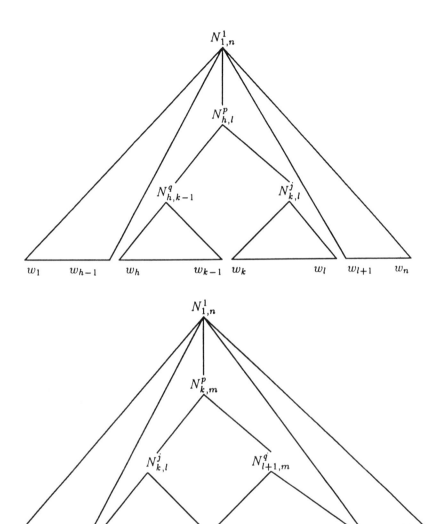

Figure 6.6
How $N_{k,l}^j$ could have arisen from larger constituents

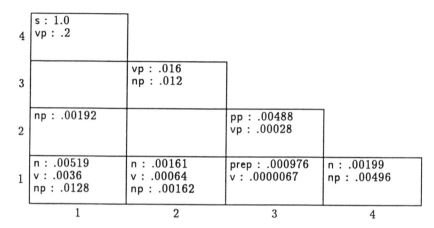

Figure 6.7
Chart and outside probabilities for "Swat flies like ants"

make the corpus as likely as possible. As the algorithm is really just a slight variation on the HMM training scheme, all of the pitfalls of the latter also show up here. In particular, our PCFG trainer finds only local maxima in the probability of the training corpus given the rule probabilities, it can get "stuck" at critical points, and, if the training corpus is unrepresentative in any way, this is reflected in unrealistic probabilities found by the training scheme.

At the topmost level, the training algorithm for HMMs given in figure 4.8 is applicable here with only the abbreviation CPFG replacing HMM. Similarly, the equation for the probabilities of the rules given the estimated counts of how often rules were used in the training corpus is a minor variation of equation 4.19. Here is the revision:

$$P_e(N^i \rightarrow \zeta^j) = \frac{C(N^i \rightarrow \zeta^j)}{\sum_k C(N^i \rightarrow \zeta^k)} \tag{6.15}$$

What does change is how we estimate the counts of how often rules are used, but even there the similarities are striking. Our derivation of the HMM training equations started by defining a transition-use count as a sum over all possible state sequences, prorated by the probability of each state sequence. We then showed how this definition was equivalent to one in which we considered instead the probability of a transition being used at a particular time tick t in the processing of the training example, and then summed over all time ticks. This was summarized in equations 4.25 and 4.26, repeated here:

$$C(s^i \overset{w^k}{\to} s^j) = \frac{1}{P(w_{1,n})} \sum_{t=1}^{n} P(S_t = s^i, S_{t+1} = s^j, W_t = w^k, w_{1,n})$$

$$= \sum_{t=1}^{n} P(s^i \overset{w^k}{\to} s^j \text{ at time tick } t \mid w_{1,n})$$

To shorten our derivation this time, we initially define our rule-use counts in a way analogous to these equations. As before, we do the formal proof for rules in Chomsky-normal form. Thus we define the counts as the sum over all positions in the chart of the probability that a constituent at that point was built up using the rule in question, or more formally,

$$C(N^j \to N^p N^q) \overset{\text{def}}{=} \sum_{k,l,m} P(N^j_{k,l}, N^p_{k,m}, N^q_{m+1,l} \mid w_{1,n})$$

$$= \frac{1}{P(w_{1,n})} \sum_{k,l,m} P(N^j_{k,l}, N^p_{k,m}, N^q_{m+1,l}, w_{1,n})$$

$$= \frac{1}{P(w_{1,n})} \sum_{k,l,m} P(w_{1,k-1}, N^j_{k,l}, w_{l+1,n}) P(N^p_{k,m}, N^q_{m+1,l} \mid N^j_{k,l})$$

$$P(w_{k,m} \mid N^p_{k,m}) P(w_{m+1,l} \mid N^q_{m+1,l})$$

$$= \frac{1}{P(w_{1,n})} \sum_{k,l,m} \alpha_j(k,l) P(N^j \to N^p N^q) \beta_p(k,m) \beta_q(m+1,l)$$

$$\tag{6.16}$$

Equation 6.16 enables us to compute the counts once we know the inside and outside probabilities of the chart constituents. It holds, of course, only for rules in Chomsky-normal form, and it does not address the question of counting the rules that introduce terminals $N^i \to w^j$. It is easy to show that for these rules the equation is

$$C(N^i \to w^j) = \frac{1}{P(w_{1,n})} \sum_{k} \alpha_i(k,k) P(N^i \to w^j, w^j = w_k). \tag{6.17}$$

We can rephrase equation 6.16 in terms of edges and in a way that does not require Chomsky-normal form rules as follows:

$$C(N^j \to \zeta^i) = \frac{1}{P(w_{1,n})} \sum_{k,l} \alpha_j(k,l) \sum_{e \in \mathcal{E}^j_{k,l}, \text{rule}(e) = N^j \to \zeta^i} \beta(e) \tag{6.18}$$

6.4   Exercises

6.1 In our algorithms for determining the inside and outside probabilities we considered the probabilities for *all* the chart constituents based upon all ways of building them up. Yet in figures 6.5 and 6.7 we included only constituents and edges used in building up the topmost s. Could any of the inside probabilities we ignored be non-zero? Could any of the outside probabilities? Explain. If either of the above answers is "yes," could the constituents omitted have any effect on the count calculations for training PCFGs?

6.2 In equation 6.14 we divide by $\beta_j(k, l)$. Give an informal argument that this term cannot be zero.

6.3 Explain why the sum over edges in equation 6.18 is not necessarily a sum over a single item. Suppose someone suggested that this term should really be a product over the edges, not a sum. Explain in intuitive terms why summing over edges makes more sense than multiplying over them.

6.4 Show that for an unambiguous parse equation 6.18 produces the expected results: each rule used in the parse gets a count of one for each time it is used.

6.5 In chart entry (1,4) of figure 6.5 two edges use the rule s → np vp. Explain how each is built up and show the calculations that lead to the edge probability for each.

6.6 What is the probability of the sentence "Swat flies like ants" according to the grammar of figure 5.1?

6.7 In our study of HMMs we presented an algorithm for finding the most likely sequence of HMM states that did not require actually considering all possible sequences of states. Find an equivalent algorithm for PCFGs. This algorithm first produces the chart parse for the sentence, along with the corresponding $\mathcal{E}_{k,l}^{j}$ and $\bar{\mathcal{E}}_{k,l}^{j}$. Then, starting at the bottom of the chart, it associates with each chart entry some information to use in building up larger chart entries. Some things to think about are: what information is needed at each chart entry, and whether this information is needed at every chart entry, or just, say, at the most probable entry at any chart location (we have implicitly answered this above, but explain why that is the correct answer).

6.8 Use the information in figures 6.5 and 6.7 to determine the count for the rule vp → verb pp when used on the sentence "Swat flies like ants."

6.9 Modify the chart parser of exercise 1.8 so that it calculates the probability of the string using the inside-probability method of equations 6.3 and 6.5. You might also want to implement the algorithm in exercise 6.7 so that your program can find the most probable parse for a sentence. Finally, if you intend to implement the inside-outside algorithm, you should extend your implementation to compute the outside probability for each constituent.

6.10 Use the chart parser of exercise 6.9 to implement a version of the PCFG-training algorithm. The best way to test your implementation is to use the corpus-generation program of exercise 1.7 to create a corpus from some context-free grammar G. Create a grammar G' that is G but with different probabilities on the rules. Give the corpus and G' to the algorithm and see how close it gets to G.

7 Learning Probabilistic Grammars

Currently we do not have a grammar for English (or any other natural language) that can handle the wide variety of sentences turning up in large corpora. This, of course, makes it impossible to apply our parsing technology to these texts. One solution to this problem would be to hire more computational linguists to develop such a grammar, but another, more interesting approach would be to try to infer a grammar from the corpus.

In chapter 5 we saw the difficulties facing those working on grammar induction. On the other hand, there are some things working in our favor as well. One of these was already noted in chapter 5—how PCFGs give us some purchase on the problem of negative training examples. But there are others as well.

For one thing, presumably much of the difficulty in classical grammar induction stems from the requirement that the grammar inducer function for any CFG. In statistical language learning the problem is different. We are not concerned with the general case. If we could simply learn a grammar for English (or at least a close context-free approximation to English), we would be quite happy, at least for a while.

Furthermore, unlike those working on the general case, we are interested in the product of the learning scheme, not just in the scheme itself. So if we can achieve our goal by putting in a few negative examples or some other hints, well, that is OK as long as it gets the job done. To put it another way, we need not hold ourselves aloof from giving our learning program "hints" as long as the burden this imposes is not too great.

We also stand to benefit in that the PCFG training scheme derived in chapter 6 suggests a very simple method for learning PCFGs, namely:

1. have the machine generate all possible PCFG rules

2. assign them some initial probabilities

3. run the training algorithm on a sample text

4. remove those rules with zero probability, leaving the "correct" grammar

The idea here is that when we generated the PCFG rules we generated right ones and wrong ones. If the training scheme does its work properly, the wrong ones should get zero probability and can thus be removed, leaving the right ones. In this chapter we look at work inspired by this simple idea.

7.1 Why the Simple Approach Fails

Unfortunately this simple idea does not work, at least not in the version stated. There are two reasons:

• Unless one places constraints on the kinds of context-free rules allowed, there is no bound on the number of possible context-free rules. A corollary to this is that, even with constraints on the number of rules, often the number is so large as to make training impractical.

• As we noted in introducing the training algorithm, this algorithm is guaranteed only to find a local maximum. That is, even if we can get all the possible rules and even if the corpus is sufficiently representative, the training algorithm can find a bad set of rules just because it found a local maximum and not the global one.

As for the first of these problems, if one does not specify the non-terminal symbols of a context-free grammar, then obviously the number of rules is unbounded since one can keep introducing new non-terminals and making up new rules for them. Thus any PCFG learner based on the above learning scheme must restrict the non-terminals to some finite set. Even if one specifies the non-terminals, the number of rules is unbounded since one can keep making up rules with longer and longer right-hand sides. So in addition the PCFG learner must impose *rule-length restrictions*.

As for the local-maximum issue, it may not be obvious at first how serious a problem this really is. However, Charniak and Carroll [11] report an experiment showing it is serious indeed. This experiment was based upon a restricted form of PCFGs so that the system was able to create all possible rules and then train the probabilities using the inside-outside algorithm. The initial probabilities for the rules were generated randomly. The purpose was to find out how many different rule sets the system would come up with when the rules were started with different probabilities—nothing else changed from run to run. The idea, of course, is that if the system produced only one set of rules, then it would seem that here, at least, there were no local maxima, while if it came up with many such sets, then there were obviously a lot of local maxima. (There is another possibility, that critical points were halting the training at places that were not even local maxima; but, as remarked in chapter 4 when discussing HMM training, introducing noise typically solves critical-point problems, and here the initial probabilities were, in a sense, *all* noise.) For the purposes of this experiment, two grammars were considered the same if they had the same set of rules and if, when the rules for a non-terminal were ordered by their probability, the ordering was the same for the two sets.

The results were unequivocal. The system was run 300 times, each time with a different random assignment of probabilities to the set of all possible rules. 300 different rule sets were found in this way. There were no duplicates.

Furthermore, in this particular case the corpus was generated by a known context-free grammar, so the probability that the correct grammar assigned to the corpus could be calculated. The correct grammar was not found in any of the 300 runs, although one run did find a very similar one that assigned the same probability to the test corpus. All of the other runs found grammars that assigned worse probabilities, and thus the training scheme was stuck 299 times in non-optimal local maxima.

We should add here that the corpus was also trained with an initial set of non-random probabilities as well, generated by counting how many times any rule could account for some local patch of a sentence. For example, in "The dog went to the park" the rule "vp → verb pp" could have been used, but the rule "vp → pp verb" could not (assuming the normal interpretations of vp and pp). These counts were then made into rule probabilities in the obvious way and training was started with these probabilities. The results were not noticeably different from those achieved with random probabilities. Thus it was not the use of random probabilities itself that somehow made the algorithm find the local maxima.

It is useful to think of our grammar learner as searching for the right probabilities in a space in which each point corresponds to a particular probability setting for each of the possible rules. If there are a lot of local maxima, then we are going to get stuck in one. Suppose, however, that we have further information on which part of the space has the true global maximum. Obviously this will help a lot. Thus, in addition to the aforementioned restrictions bounding the number of rules, we also require this rule-space information. The most obvious kind of rule-space information is a further restriction on the kinds of rules allowed. This would be equivalent to knowledge that certain of .e probabilities in the larger search space must be zero (since the rules are no longer allowed). However, as we show in the following discussion, there are many ways to give some guidance in our search through the rule space.

In what follows we look at three experiments that differ primarily in their use of extra information to guide the training algorithm. We will see that there is a good correlation between the strength of the information provided and the results achieved. We present the work in order of increasing guidance.

7.2   Learning Dependency Grammars

Carroll and Charniak [11,12] built a grammar-induction program in which the constraint on rules came from the program's restriction to *dependency grammars.* A dependency grammar is, in essence, just an $\overline{\mathrm{X}}$ grammar (see section 1.3) in which only one level of barred categories is allowed. Formally, a dependency grammar is a triple $< N, S, R >$ where S is the start symbol for the rewrite rules and N a set of parts of speech (which in effect act like terminal symbols) $\{n^1, \ldots, n^\omega\}$; R is a set of rewrite rules that is a subset of the set defined as follows: $\{S \rightarrow \overline{n} \mid n \in N\} \cup \{\overline{n} \rightarrow \alpha n \beta \mid n \in N, \alpha, \beta \in \Gamma\}$, where Γ is the set of strings of zero or more $\overline{a}$, for $a \in N$. Such a rewrite system produces a tree structure in the normal way. For example, figure 7.1 gives a dependency-grammar phrase marker for the sentence "She ate the hamburger with a fork." Furthermore, for the purposes of the grammar-learning experiments the right-hand sides of rules were arbitrarily limited to be of maximum length four. Thus there is only a finite number of possible rules.

One major difference between the work in this section and the two projects that follow is that the present work takes a more incremental approach to grammar learning. Rather than creating all of the possible rules (subject to the constraints) and then training them on the corpus, here the rules are created only when a sentence is found that cannot be parsed using the existing grammar. More specifically, when a sentence is encountered that cannot be parsed with the current grammar, *all* rules that are applicable to the sentence at hand are added to the grammar and the resulting grammar is retrained on all of the sentences seen so far. Furthermore, the corpus was sorted by sentence length, with the idea that it would be easier to learn a grammar for shorter sentences than longer ones, and that the short-sentence grammar could be extended to longer sentences by adding rules as needed. This algorithm is summarized in figure 7.2.

We noted earlier the distinction between positive and negative training examples. It is interesting to note that in dealing with PCFGs this distinction can be finessed somewhat. For example, suppose a grammar assigns a relatively high probability to the sentence $w_{1,n}$, but this sentence does not appear in the corpus. (This is more plausible if we assume that $w_{1,n}$ are parts of speech and not actual words.) The probability of this happening in a corpus of m sentences is

$$(1 - P(w_{1,n}))^m \tag{7.1}$$

Charniak and Carroll's system [11,12] has a threshold on this number such that, when the probability falls below the threshold, the system "considers" the possibility that this sentence really is not in the grammar, or at least

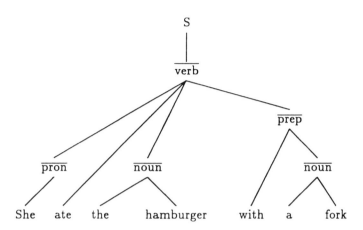

Figure 7.1
Tree-structure version of a dependency-grammar parse

grammar = {};
Loop for s_i = the ith sentence in the corpus sorted by length;
    If grammar can parse s_i, continue;
    Else grammar = grammar ∪ rules-for(s_i));
        Retrain grammar on $s_1, \ldots, s_i$;
Return grammar;

Figure 7.2
Algorithm for training on a sorted corpus

not nearly as likely as the current grammar makes out. This in turn is taken as evidence that at least one of the current rules used in the parse of this sentence is incorrect. To test this possibility, the system records the current cross entropy and then tries eliminating each of the rules in turn. In each case the grammar is trained with other (possibly new) rules for parsing the corpus sentences. If the cross entropy of any of these trials is below the original "current" cross entropy, then the grammar that produced the lowest of these is adopted as the new grammar.

While using the probabilistic information to get, in effect, negative examples from a corpus has a certain elegance, there is some question about its usefulness. The problem is that $P(w_{1,n})$ must be reasonably high before the term in equation 7.1 is low enough to suggest a rule might be wrong. For example, if we set the threshold at .3 (that is, only 30% of the time would we see the corpus without this sentence) and if our corpus is a large one, say a million sentences, then it is possible to show that the probability of the sentence in question must be at least $1.2 \cdot 10^{-6}$. This may not seem very large, but it is. For example, if we had ten parts of speech, all equally likely, then any sentence with more than six parts of speech would have too low a probability. Thus any such sentences must be very short, and there is some debate about how much good they can do. But they do seem to do some good for the system we are discussing here.

Nevertheless, as mentioned in the previous section, without any further guidance the grammars constructed are very unintuitive; figure 7.3 shows the eight most probable expansions for $\overline{\text{pron}}$ found by the system after seeing sentences of up to length eight from an artificial corpus created from a very simple dependency grammar.

The constraints added to prod the system into the correct area of the probability parameter space are mild compared to the systems discussed in the next two sections. In particular, this work constrained only the non-terminals that could appear in each of the other non-terminal's rules. For example, one could add the constraint that no other non-terminals could be part of an expansion of $\overline{\text{pron}}$. A strong restriction like this would preclude all of the rules in figure 7.3, and would, in fact, only allow one rule for expanding $\overline{\text{pron}}$, namely $\overline{\text{pron}} \rightarrow$ pron. Indeed, it was found that very simple grammars could be learned with a few restrictions of this form. (In the above case, simply disallowing $\overline{\text{verb}}$ in the expansion of $\overline{\text{pron}}$ was sufficient to avoid all the spurious pronoun rules.)

This system was tried only on comparatively simple corpora generated from simple hand-written dependency grammars (the most complicated grammar had 48 rules). It was able to learn this and the two simpler ones up to minor variations in the probabilities associated with each rule.

7.3   Learning from a Bracketed Corpus

One interesting way to force the initial probabilities into the correct part of the parameter space was proposed by Pereira and Schabes [35]. They started with a Chomsky-normal-form grammar consisting of 45 part-of-speech symbols (which they took as the terminal symbols for their experiment) and a set of 15 non-terminal symbols. Thus the number of possible rules is fixed at $15 \times 45 = 675$ rules of the form $N^i \rightarrow w^j$ and $15 \times 15 \times 15 = 3375$ rules of the form $N^i \rightarrow N^p \, N^q$, for a total of 4050 rules. These rules were trained

.220	$\overline{pron}$	→	pron $\overline{verb}$	.117	$\overline{pron}$	→	$\overline{det\ verb}$ pron
.214	$\overline{pron}$	→	$\overline{prep}$ pron	.038	$\overline{pron}$	→	pron $\overline{verb}$ $\overline{noun}$
.139	$\overline{pron}$	→	pron $\overline{verb\ det}$	.023	$\overline{pron}$	→	$\overline{noun\ verb}$ pron
.118	$\overline{pron}$	→	$\overline{verb}$ pron	.013	$\overline{pron}$	→	pron $\overline{verb\ det\ det}$

Figure 7.3
Some expansions for $\overline{pron}$ found by the unrestricted system

on 770 sentences (7812 words) that were not raw but *bracketed*. That is, the terminal symbols of a sentence were grouped together into the higher-level constituents, but the names of the higher-level constituents were omitted. This scheme also allows *partial bracketing*, in which some but not all of the groupings are indicated. For example, figure 7.4 shows the full parse tree for (one parse of) the sentence "Salespeople sold the dog biscuits." A full bracketing, partial bracketing, and full bracketing using the parts of speech (which are what this program sees) look like this:

((Salespeople (sold (the dog biscuits))) .   )
(Salespeople (sold   the dog biscuits)   .   )
((noun   (verb (det noun noun))) fpunc)

What Pereira and Schabes realized is that even partial bracketing information can give guidance to the PCFG training algorithm. To see how this works, remember that our training scheme computes for each possible place in our chart the probability that the rule was used to create a non-terminal at that chart location, and then sums over all chart locations. Of course, these probabilities are the probabilities given the observed words in the sentence. We now want to do the same thing—that is, compute the probability that the rule is used at each chart location—but given the observed words and the observed bracketing. For example, suppose we want to know the probability that a rule like vp → noun verb creates a length-two constituent starting at word one in the sentence "Salespeople sold the dog biscuits." If we had no bracketing information then such a constituent would be possible, but with the partial bracketing (noun (verb det noun noun) fpunc), and obviously with the full bracketing as well, it is not possible because it goes over the brackets (that is, it would have to be made up of fragments of two or more groups). While a non-terminal can span two or more complete brackets, as in (noun verb det noun verb), and while a non-terminal can span only some

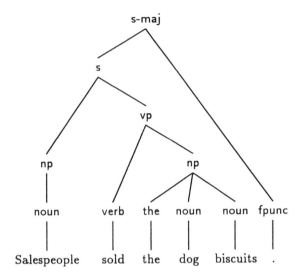

Figure 7.4
A parse tree to illustrate bracketing

of the fragments of a partial bracketing, as in (det noun), any non-terminal that goes over a bracketing boundary and does not include all of the bracket is not compatible with the bracketing, as in (noun verb).

With this in mind, we can return to the equation derived in chapter 6 for estimating the counts for how many (prorated) times a rule $N^j \rightarrow N^p N^q$ is used in a certain sentence, equation 6.16, repeated here:

$$C(N^j \rightarrow N^p N^q) = \frac{1}{P(w_{1,n})} \sum_{k,l,m} \alpha_j(k,l) P(N^j \rightarrow N^p N^q) \beta_p(k,m) \beta_q(m+1,l)$$

(Again, this is for the Chomsky-normal form, which is the form used in [35].) We do not go through the formal derivation to introduce the bracketing information, but instead simply give the new version:

$$C(N^j \rightarrow N^p N^q) = \frac{1}{P(w_{1,n}, brackets)}$$
$$\sum_{k,l,m} b(k,l) \alpha_j(k,l) P(N^j \rightarrow N^p N^q) b(k,m) \beta_p(k,m)$$
$$b(m+1,l) \beta_q(m+1,l) \qquad (7.2)$$

Here we have first conditionalized the probability on both the words and the brackets, and then added several calls to the function $b(k, l)$ defined as:

$$b(k, l) = \begin{cases} 1 & \text{if } N_{k,l} \text{ is consistent with bracketing} \\ 0 & \text{otherwise} \end{cases} \tag{7.3}$$

The idea is that this function eliminates any possible contribution to the count from a rule application that would not be consistent with the brackets. In particular, since in equation 7.2 we wish to get the counts by summing over the contributions of the rule applications $N_{k,l}^j \to N_{k,m}^p N_{m+1,l}^q$, we use the bracketing function three times, once for each of the three non-terminals, to make sure that they are consistent with the bracketing.

The results are much as one would expect. The algorithm was trained on 700 sentences from a corpus of 770 sentences and then tested on the unseen 70. The resulting grammar was used to assign a most-probable parse to each text using a PCFG adaptation of the Viterbi algorithm for the most probable sequence of HMM states. The resulting parse was judged simply by how well it assigned the full brackets to the test sentences. (If you think about it, the particular non-terminals it assigned are not meaningful since, even if we gave them meaningful names, the fact that the system started out with all possible rules means that there was no way to, say, make vp correspond to what we normally think of as a verb phrase any more than to what we normally think of as a prepositional phrase, or anything else.) When the input did not contain the brackets, the resulting brackets were correct only 37% of the time. When bracketing information was included this went up to 90%. Interestingly, while training increased performance for the bracketed corpus from 37% to 90%, it did not improve performance for the unbracketed corpus at all. This fact seems significant, but its interpretation is not obvious.

7.4 Improving a Partial Grammar

Of the three approaches described here, Briscoe and Waegner's [7] applies the greatest restrictions on the grammar in order to avoid local maxima. Perhaps because of this, their method creates the most realistic grammars of the three.

Briscoe and Waegner start with the constraint that the grammar be in Chomsky-normal form with a restricted number of non-terminal symbols. They also explicitly adopt a version of $\overline{X}$ theory in which two levels of bars are permitted. In order to tie down, say, $\overline{\overline{noun}}$ to phrases in which nouns appear, rules have the following restrictions:

1. In the rule $\overline{x} \rightarrow y\ z$, either y or z must be either an x or an $\overline{x}$

2. In the rule $\overline{\overline{x}} \rightarrow y\ z$, either y or z must be an x, an $\overline{x}$ or an $\overline{\overline{x}}$

Thus, for example, both $\overline{noun}$ and $\overline{\overline{noun}}$ when expanded by these rules eventually expand into phrases containing at least one noun. Note, however, that double-barred non-terminals are not restricted to expand into single-barred ones that in turn expand into parts of speech and hence into words. For example, in this scheme pronouns are $\overline{\overline{nouns}}$, as in "$\overline{\overline{noun}} \rightarrow$ he." This makes sense if one thinks of a $\overline{\overline{noun}}$ as a complete noun phrase.

Briscoe and Waegner place a second restriction on their rules, the import of which is much less clear: in any rule of the form "$x \rightarrow y\ z$" in which both y and z are parts of speech (i.e., have zero bars), z must be either an adverb or a noun. One thing we have not discussed is the fact that in $\overline{X}$ theory most words are classified as having the features of ±noun and ±verb. Nouns are +noun and −verb, whereas adverbs are +noun and +verb. The reasons for this are beyond the scope of our text. However, it does serve to make the otherwise odd conjunction of nouns and adverbs in this second restriction slightly more reasonable, since the rule actually says that z must be +noun.

However, even with all of these constraints, the total system is probably still more general than the dependency grammar formalism used by Carroll and Charniak [11,12]. As we saw, just assuming a dependency grammar is not sufficient to get reasonable results. Thus by themselves these constraints on $\overline{X}$ rules are unlikely to let the rules train to a reasonable grammar. Briscoe and Waegner's truly major restriction is to give the system a partial grammar to start from. For example, in one preliminary experiment they started with the grammar in figure 7.5. The only new part of speech introduced here are the degree words, such as "so," "too," and "very." One can start the system with such a grammar "built in" in several ways, probably the easiest being to give the rules of the built-in grammar extra counts that are independent of the actual examples used for training. So, for example, we could add, say, 50 or 100 to the count for the rule $\overline{verb} \rightarrow \overline{noun}$ verb. This, of course, makes this rule more likely, but more importantly, it affects the other rules in the system. At the most obvious level, suppose there is a competing rule $\overline{\overline{noun}}$ $\rightarrow \overline{noun}$ verb. The probability added to its competitor causes sentences to

verb	→	noun verb		noun	→	det noun
verb	→	verb noun		noun	→	noun prep
verb	→	verb adverb		prep	→	prep noun
adverb	→	degree adverb				

Figure 7.5
A sample Chomsky-normal-form "starter" grammar

use verb → noun verb whenever possible as that rule has "artificially" high probability, which in turn makes the probability of the sentence higher.

A more ambitious experiment started with a grammar used to parse the SEC corpus, a 50,000-word corpus transcribed from radio programs. This grammar was able to parse about 25% of the corpus. With this grammar as a seed, all of the possible rules that obeyed the above two constraints were then added to the already existing parts of speech and other non-terminal symbols. This system was then trained and zero-probability rules were removed. The result was a system that was able to parse about 75% of the corpus.

To get some idea of how well the system does, as well as the kinds of difficulties that real-life corpora pose, it is instructive to consider one of the sentences it could parse. To fit it on the page we have broken the parse tree into the four parts shown in figures 7.6 and 7.7: the first three parts are the three main constituents of the sentence, while the fourth is the top of the tree that connects these three constituents.

While the overall structure of the parse is correct, there are a few errors. Of these, the most striking, because the least explicable, is in the first tree in figure 7.7, where the system splits up the obvious noun phrase "our time" by making a prepositional phrase "in our" and using "time" in a very funny noun phrase whose topmost constituents are "Mr Moon time." This is strange because it requires what one would imagine to be a very unlikely rule, prep → prep det.

There are other mistakes as well, but these are somewhat less puzzling. It is generally recognized that the major influence on prepositional-phrase attachment is semantic in nature; syntax provides only the loosest constraints on the process. Thus it is not too surprising that the parse mistakenly attaches the prepositional phrase headed by "in" in the first tree of figure 7.6 to "award" rather than "announcing." Similarly, syntax provides little guidance on noun-noun modification. For example, should "bird feeder kit" be parsed

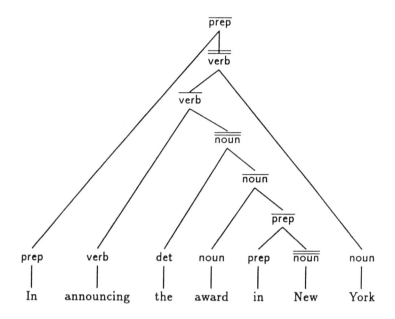

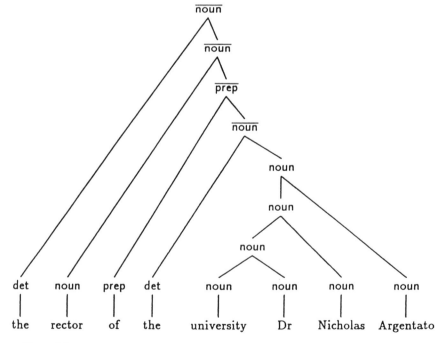

Figure 7.6
A complicated parse tree with mistakes—Part 1

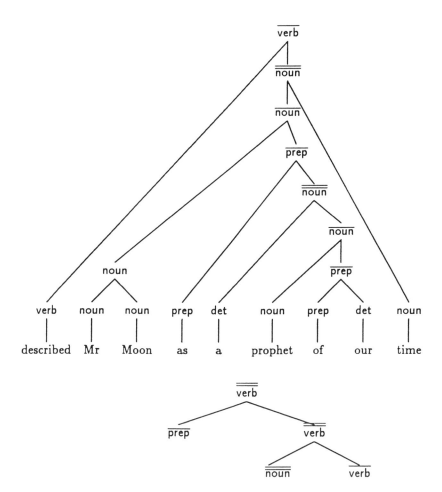

Figure 7.7
A complicated parse tree with mistakes—Part 2

as ((bird feeder) kit) or (bird (feeder kit))? The former makes more sense, but
the alternate bracketing is correct for "adult library card." The cases of mis-
placed noun-noun modifications in figures 7.7 and 7.6 are admittedly more
extreme. For example, the system split up "Dr Nicholas Argentato" but combined "university Dr" into a phrase. Presumably if the tag set distinguished
honorifics and proper nouns from regular nouns it could have gotten this one
right, but in general the problem is hard. Similarly for the mistake with "New
York." Thus it is probably not all that relevant how many mistakes there are

in the most likely parse, as syntax in general does not have the information needed to make the right decision. So if the correct parse were, say, in second place, and only modestly behind the most likely, then the grammar would still be doing a good job.

This suggests that probability might be a better measure of parser performance than percentage of correct attachments. This in turn suggests two possible measures. Suppose we are testing a grammar G on a test set of m sentences $s_{1,m}$, and let $t_{1,m}$ be the correct parses of $s_{1,m}$. Consider the two measures M_1 and M_2:

$$M_1(G, s_{1,m}) \stackrel{\text{def}}{=} -\log \prod_{j=1}^{m} P(t_j \mid s_j) \qquad (7.4)$$

$$M_2(G, s_{1,m}) \stackrel{\text{def}}{=} -\frac{1}{n} \log \prod_{j=1}^{m} P(s_j, t_j) \qquad (7.5)$$

The difference between M_1 and M_2 is that the first normalizes the probability by dividing by the probability of the sentences according to the grammar, whereas the second just normalizes by dividing the logarithm by the number of words (or, equivalently, by dividing the probability $P(s_j, t_j)$ by 2^n). While the two measures are obviously similar, they can differ significantly. In particular, M_1 is more forgiving of a grammar that assigns low probability to all of the parses of a sentence, provided that G assigns the right parse the highest probability. M_2, on the other hand, would rather that the right parse have a high probability, even if not the highest. Either one, however, is probably a better measure than correct attachment percentage.

7.5 Exercises

7.1 Specify a context-free language L and two grammars G_1 and G_2 with the following properties:

• the languages of G_1 and G_2 are both supersets of L (though not necessarily proper supersets)

• when run on a representative corpus of sentences from L, G_1 performs better than G_2 according to the measure M_1 in equation 7.4, while G_2 does better according to M_2 in equation 7.5

7.2 Write a program that automatically generates all possible dependency grammar rules for a given set of parts of speech and a restriction on the length of the right-hand side of a rule. Using the program of exercise 1.7, generate an artificial tagged corpus for a grammar that has as its rule set a known subset of the rules just created. You are now in a position to perform the experiment described in section 7.1 to see how the results after training are a function of the starting probabilities. (Note that you need to give some thought to how to generate "random" probability distributions for this experiment.)

7.3 Repeat the experiments of exercise 7.2, but this time use an artificial bracketed corpus and train using the equations that take bracketing into account, equations 7.2 and 7.3. (Your author has not done this experiment. If you do it, please let me known what happens. One would expect that the bracketing would be sufficient to determine the correct grammar.)

8 Syntactic Disambiguation

The last chapter ended with the observation that syntax by itself does not have the information necessary to decide correctly on the intended parse of a syntactically ambiguous sentence. While a PCFG assigns higher probability to parses that use common constructions than to those with less common ones, frequently the differences can be small and the deciding information lies elsewhere. We remarked on this briefly in chapter 5 and noted there how prepositional-phrase attachment is particularly difficult for purely grammatical approaches because prepositional phrases attach to noun or verb phrases with approximately equal probability, as in:

Sue bought a plant with Jane.

Sue bought a plant with yellow leaves.

Normally when syntactic information becomes insufficient one invokes "meaning" as the deciding factor and leaves surface phenomena, like words, behind. With our statistical approach we cannot be so cavalier. As this chapter shows, however, it is possible to make progress in this area with statistical methods.

8.1 Simple Methods for Prepositional Phrases

We start with our prototype problem—prepositional-phrase attachment. In particular, we consider only sentences of the form "verb np_1 (prep np_2)." The question is whether the pp, (prep np_2), attaches to verb or np_1. We call this the attachment decision. To keep things simple, we assume that the attachment decision is independent of anything other than prep, verb, np_1 and np_2. More formally, let A be a random variable representing this attachment decision. As such it can take one of two values, verb if the pp attaches to the verb, and np_1 if to the noun. Let w be the words in the text outside of "verb np_1 (prep np_2)". We assume

$$P(A \mid \text{prep}, \text{verb}, np_1, np_2, w) = P(A \mid \text{prep}, \text{verb}, np_1, np_2) \qquad (8.1)$$

This assumption is, as one might guess, false. For example, our normal interpretation of "Fred saw a movie with Arnold Schwarzenegger" is that "with Arnold Schwarzenegger" modifies "movie," not "saw." Yet had this been preceded by a story about how Mr. Schwarzenegger found himself in a small town with nothing to do and struck up a conversation with Fred, the bellhop at the hotel, our interpretation would be different. Nevertheless, the assumption is not a bad one and, given our current abilities, we have no choice but to make it.

However, if we hope to collect statistics, the assumption in equation 8.1 is not sufficient, since the noun phrases np_1 and np_2 can be arbitrarily complicated and the number of noun phrases we encounter makes it impossible to collect complete statistics on them. Thus we next assume that the only thing relevant in a noun phrase is the head noun. For example, in "Sue bought a plant with yellow leaves" the only relevant aspect of "a plant" is "plant" and of "yellow leaves" is "leaves." Again, not correct, but not unreasonable. Thus if $noun_1$ and $noun_2$ are the heads of np_1 and np_2 respectively, we assume that

$$P(A \mid \text{prep}, \text{verb}, np_1, np_2, noun_1, noun_2) = P(A \mid \text{prep}, \text{verb}, noun_1, noun_2)$$
(8.2)

Unfortunately, this is still far from being something for which we can collect statistics. Assume English has 10^4 nouns, 10^4 verbs, and 10 prepositions. (As the Brown corpus has about $5 \cdot 10^4$ word types in all and most of them are nouns and verbs, this estimate is low but reasonable for quick calculations.) Then the total number of combinations would be 10^{13}. Obviously further simplifications are required. First, let us assume that the propensity of the pp to attach to verb or $noun_1$ can be summarized by statistics on its propensity to attach to verb versus its propensity to attach to $noun_1$. That is, statistics on how often pp attaches to verb (independent of any possible $noun_1$ attachment) and how often pp attaches to $noun_1$ (independent of what verb might be around) would suffice for making our decisions. More formally, let $f(p, n, a)$ be some measure of how much a prepositional phrase with preposition p and head noun n wants to attach to a—either a verb or a head noun of a noun phrase. Then we assume that

$$P(A = \text{noun} \mid \text{prep}, \text{verb}, noun_1, noun_2)$$
$$> P(A = \text{verb} \mid \text{prep}, \text{verb}, noun_1, noun_2)$$
$$\Leftrightarrow f(\text{prep}, noun_2, noun_1) > f(\text{prep}, noun_2, \text{verb}) \qquad (8.3)$$

Thus we need to collect not one set of (as many as) 10^{13} parameters, but two sets of (as many as) 10^9 parameters—one set on how much the prepositional phrase likes the verb and another on how much it likes the noun. This is obviously an improvement, but just as obviously not good enough.

At this point there are two ways to go. One is to condition our probabilities on fewer things. Another would be to condition the probabilities on
more general things, so we would need statistics for fewer cases. Presumably
these generalizations would be semantic in nature. We consider each of these
possibilities in turn.

One experiment done in this vein is that by Hindle and Rooth [28].
Their solution to the sparse-data problem was to make a further simplifying assumption—namely, that the head noun of the prepositional phrase has
no effect on the probabilities. This is not a very good assumption, but it can
be argued that, if the remaining information can be collected, it is better than
nothing at all. Thus they are assuming that

$$P(A \mid \text{prep}, \text{verb}, \text{noun}_1, \text{noun}_2) = P(A \mid \text{prep}, \text{verb}, \text{noun}_1) \qquad (8.4)$$

and then that

$$P(A = \text{noun} \mid \text{prep}, \text{verb}, \text{noun}_1) > P(A = \text{verb} \mid \text{prep}, \text{verb}, \text{noun}_1)$$
$$\Leftrightarrow f(\text{prep}, \text{noun}_1) > f(\text{prep}, \text{verb}). \qquad (8.5)$$

At this point the problem is reduced to collecting two sets of data upon which
to calculate $f(\text{prep}, \text{noun}_1)$ and $f(\text{prep}, \text{verb})$. Each set has a size on the order
of 10^5—large, but not impossible. In particular, Hindle and Rooth take

$$f(\text{prep}, \text{verb}) = P(\text{prep} \mid \text{verb}) \qquad (8.6)$$

$$f(\text{prep}, \text{noun}) = P(\text{prep} \mid \text{noun}) \qquad (8.7)$$

Naturally we estimate these with the counts

$$P(\text{prep} \mid \text{verb}) \approx \frac{C(\text{prep attached to verb})}{C(\text{verb})} \qquad (8.8)$$

and similarly for nouns.

We then need to get the counts. $C(\text{verb})$ is easy. $C(\text{prep attached to verb})$ is
harder because a lot of the relevant data is itself subject to the very ambiguity
we wish to resolve. That is, often we find sentences in the corpus of the form
"verb np_1 (prep np_2)" and, since we do not know where the prepositional
phrase (prep np_2) attaches, we cannot collect the statistics. The solution is
that sometimes we can figure this out and we hope this is sufficient. So the
program first puts the corpus through a parser that attempts to find places
where a prepositional phrase follows a noun phrase, a verb, or both. The
parser, however, makes no assumptions about the attachment point. Hindle

and Rooth then estimate the pp attachment counts in (more or less) the following manner:

1. if a noun is followed by a pp but there is no preceding verb, increment C(prep attached to noun). This happens, for example, if the noun is the subject of the sentence.

2. if a passive verb is followed by a pp other than a "by" phrase, increment C(prep attached to verb), e.g., "The dog was hit on the leg." (The paper does not discuss other verb-pp combinations such as "Sue ate in the park," though one would imagine these should be handled in the same way.)

3. if a pp follows both a noun phrase and a verb but the noun phrase is a pronoun, increment C(prep attached to verb), e.g., "Sue saw him in the park."

4. if a pp follows both a noun and a verb, see if the probabilities based upon the attachments decided by rules 1-3 greatly favor one or the other attachment. If so, increment that count. The test used to decide if the probabilities "greatly favor" is the t-score (see below).

5. otherwise increment both attachment counters by .5.

For those not familiar with t-scores (mentioned in step 4 above), a word of explanation is in order. The t-score is a standard test to see if the results could be expected on the basis of chance. That is, suppose we are trying to decide if a preposition p attaches to a verb v or a noun n. One straightforward thing to do is to compare conditional probabilities, as in

$$P(p \mid n) - P(p \mid v). \tag{8.9}$$

If this is positive we guess that p attaches to n, if negative, to v. However, the probabilities in question may be so close and the evidence so meager that we should not guess, or should at least recognize that our guess is based upon unreliable data. More formally, we ask: What is the chance that we would have observed this difference in probabilities if the difference really had been zero? Obviously, if the chance is low then we reject the hypothesis (called the null hypothesis, where "null" means "no difference"). "Low" is typically taken as less that 1 chance in 20, or 5%. A measure of this is given by the so-called *t-score*:

$$t \stackrel{\text{def}}{=} \frac{P(p \mid n) - P(p \mid v)}{\sqrt{\sigma^2 P(p \mid n) + \sigma^2 P(p \mid v)}} \tag{8.10}$$

Here the numerator is just the simple idea we had before but the denominator is a factor intended to measure the significance of the data. In particular, σ is a measure of how reliable the data is. In [28] the following approximation is made:

$$\sigma^2 = 1/C(n) \qquad (8.11)$$

That is, the reliability of the data goes up with the square root of the amount of data we have (we do not go into the reasons for this approximation here). The t-score measures the likelihood of the null hypothesis. In Hindle and Root's case, an absolute value of 1.65 or greater is taken to mean that the probability of the null hypothesis is $\leq 5\%$. Obviously, the sign of the score tells us which way to guess.

The results obtained in this experiment are shown in figure 8.1. The first row shows how well it is possible to do simply by always picking the noun attachment (which was the more common one). This gives a baseline for judging performance. The next line, showing how well two people did when given just the information available to the program, suggests that limited information does degrade one's ability to perform the task. (The judges are presumed to have 100% accuracy with total information, since human intuition was the "gold standard" for deciding the correct answer.) The third line shows the performance of the program. While it is an improvement on, say, always picking a noun attachment, it is clearly worse than human performance.

A possible reason for this is suggested by the fourth line, which shows how well the program does if we consider only those examples for which it had enough data to put the t-score result at the 95% level. On these examples its performance was virtually the same as that of the human judges. The final line gives human performance on the subset of examples for which the program's data was sufficient to put it at the 95% level. This result indicates that this restricted set of examples was not special in some way that made it easier: the human judges' results on the restricted set were not significantly better than on the full set. This suggests that sparse data was a major cause of the difference between the human judges' performance and that of the program.

8.2   Using Semantic Information

The results of the previous section strongly suggest that limiting the information about the prepositional phrase to simply its preposition is insufficient for very accurate attachment decisions. Yet we have already noted the effect

	Choose noun	Choose verb	Percent correct
Choose noun	889	0	64.0
2 human judges	551	338	85.7
Program	565	354	78.1
Program > 95%	407	201	85.0
Humans > 95%	416	192	86.9

Figure 8.1
Results of prepositional-phrase attachment

of sparse data on Hindle and Rooth's results [28]. It seems possible that a larger effort to collect appropriate data would give a more reasonable estimate on the 10^5 or so data points required. However, collecting data for the 10^9 data points required if we were to condition also on the head noun in the prepositional phrase does not seem practical, even if most of probabilities are effectively zero.

One solution to this problem is to condition not on the head nouns (nor, for that matter, on the verb) but rather on *semantic tags* associated with them. For example, we might label "artist," "Jane," "plumber," "Ted" as human, "Friday," "June," "yesterday" as time, "hammer," "leaves," "pot" as object, and so on. This particular classification is somewhat arbitrary, but one can see how to use it to distinguish the two attachment problems given at the start of this chapter:

Sue bought a plant with Jane.

Sue bought a plant with yellow leaves.

Presumably we would find that prepositional phrases of the form "with human" tend to attach more to the verb of the sentence, while those "with object" might attach more to other nouns. The fact that there would be many fewer semantic categories than words could substantially reduce the sparse-data problem, though admittedly at the cost of determining the semantic labels.

Experiments in this vein were performed by Basili et al. [4]. Like Hindle and Rooth, they extracted simple syntactic relationships, particularly those of the form "verb pp," "np pp," and "verb np pp." They too then used the unambiguous cases to determine preference attachments. However, they also manually associated with the nouns and verbs in the lexicon semantic tags tailored to the domain of discourse. They had corpora for two such domains, commercial and legal. We consider only their data for the commercial corpus, for which the semantic tags were: physical_act, mental_act, artifact, human_entity, vegetable, building, by_product, matter, animals, machine, and places. Their first experiment gathered the statistics on the preposition, the semantic tag of the head noun in the prepositional phrase and the semantic tag of either the verb or the noun attachment location. For example, "ate at the restaurant" would be classified as "physical_act at building." In particular, they gathered the following statistic:

$$\frac{C(\text{attach\_semantic\_class, prep, pp\_noun\_semantic\_class})}{C(\text{prep})} \tag{8.129}$$

Here "attach_semantic_class" is the semantic class of the possible noun or verb attachment points. (While the paper discusses collecting other syntactic relations and defines equation 8.12 for relations other than prepositional-phrase attachment, all the examples in the experiments described involve prepositional-phrase attachment.) In terms of our earlier formalization, they assume that

$$P(A = \text{noun} \mid \text{prep}, \text{verb}, \text{noun}_1, \text{noun}_2)$$
$$> P(A = \text{verb} \mid \text{prep}, \text{verb}, \text{noun}_1, \text{noun}_2)$$
$$\Leftrightarrow f(\text{prep}, S(\text{noun}_2), S(\text{noun}_1)) > f(\text{prep}, S(\text{noun}_2), S(\text{verb})) \tag{8.130}$$

where $S(x)$ is the semantic tag of x and where

$$f(\text{prep}, S(\text{noun}_2), S(\text{verb})) = P(S(\text{noun}_2), S(\text{verb}) \mid \text{prep})$$

They then restrict consideration to those triples "attach_semantic_class, prep, pp_noun_semantic_class" for which equation 8.12 is higher than some system-defined threshold T. For example, figure 8.2 shows significant triples involving the Italian preposition "da" (the corpora for this work were in Italian).

One might expect the attachments to be decided on the basis of which of the noun or verb maximized equation 8.12, but this is not the case. For some reason the authors chose the following algorithm. If only one of the equation 8.12 conditional probabilities is above the threshold, choose it, otherwise do not decide. This means that when the algorithm makes a decision it does a good job, but that quite often it cannot make a choice. Thus, it makes a choice in only 49% of the cases, but it is right 85% of the time.

Attachment location semantics	Prep	Head noun semantics	Italian example	English translation
artifact	da	artifact	biancheria da letta	linens for bed
physical_act	da	human_entity	venduto da i soci	sold by the shareholders
artifact	da	place	articoli da spiaggia	items for beach
physical_act	da	building	comprare da oleifici	buy from oil refineries

Figure 8.2
Significant semantic pairs for the Italian preposition "da"

It is not clear from the data if the inability to choose 51% of the time is primarily because neither attachment possibility was above the t-score threshold, or because both were. If the latter, then it would make sense to make the attachment rules more specific so as to get fewer cases of conflicting advice. This is, in fact, what the authors did. Rather than collecting "semantic_tag preposition semantic_tag" triples, they now collected "word preposition semantic_tag" triples. They also changed the choice mechanism to force a choice in every case. Now their system made the correct choice only 75% of the time, but now, of course, it did not abstain. Interestingly, this result is quite close to that of Hindle and Rooth, where no semantic information about the noun in the prepositional phrase was available. On the other hand, much less training data was available in this study, which presumably had a negative impact on the results.

8.3 Relative-Clause Attachment

Another source of syntactic ambiguity is the attachment of relative clauses. Consider the following examples:

(1) Fred awarded a prize to the dog and Bill, who trained it.

(2) Fred awarded a prize to Sue and Fran, who sang a great song.

(3) Fred awarded a prize for penmanship that was worth $50.00.

(4) Fred awarded a prize for the dog that ran the fastest.

Each of these sentences has a relative clause (e.g., "who trained it") headed by a relative pronoun (e.g., "who"). In the first of these sentences the relative clause attaches to the noun phrase "Bill," while in the second it attaches not to "Fran" but rather to the noun phrase "Sue and Fran." Similarly the "that" in the third example attaches to "prize," while in the fourth the "that" attaches to "dog."

Often a distinction is made between *restrictive relative clauses* and *unrestrictive relative clauses*. Example (4) above is the former, while (1–3) are the latter. The difference is that a restrictive relative restricts consideration to a subclass: example (4) restricts "the dog" to be the one that ran the fastest. An unrestrictive relative clause, on the other hand, just adds more information without making any further restrictions. For example, in (1) "who trained it" gives us more information about "Bill" but does not restrict "Bill." We mention this distinction because it is a common one and readers aware of it may think it affects our problem. In fact, it does not seem to, as either way we need to figure out where the phrase attaches. Figure 8.3 shows what the attachment would look like for sentence (2).

The problem of deciding where a relative pronoun attaches is addressed in work by Fisher and Riloff [19]. They characterize the problem as one of determining the referent of the relative pronoun, but since a relative pronoun always refers to the noun phrase to which it is attached, this is equivalent to deciding on the attachment location, which is how we frame it here.

The clause following any relative pronoun has a *gap* that is the position tacitly filled by the relative pronoun. Consider the three examples

the dog that ate the cookie

the dog that Sue bought

the dog that Fred gave the biscuit to

In the first of these, "the dog" is the subject of "ate the cookie," in the second it is the direct object of "bought," and in the third it is the noun phrase of the prepositional phrase "to the dog." Thus one problem with relative pronouns is

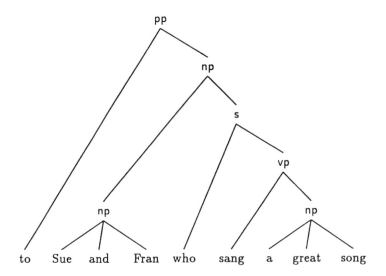

Figure 8.3
Attachment for a relative pronoun

deciding where the head noun fits into the relative clause. Interestingly, in all the examples found by Fisher and Riloff the noun phrase serves as the subject of the relative clause, and that is the only case they handle. However, they do find examples in which the relative clause is passive; that is, the entity in the subject position is logically the direct object and the noun phrase provided by a "by" prepositional phrase, if such a phrase exists, is the sentence's logical subject. For example,

Sue ate a cookie that was baked by Fran.

In this example logically it is Fran who baked the cookie.

Since we can assume that the head noun serves as the subject of the relative clause, the obvious source of information to guide the attachment decision is how well the various potential attachment noun phrases could serve as the syntactic subject of the clause. Thus, for the relative clause "who baked a cookie" we would prefer a noun like "Sam" to a noun like "telephone" as the attachment point, since Sam could bake a better cookie than a telephone could. Similarly, if the lower sentence is passive, "that was baked by Sam," we would prefer "cookie" to "Fred."

Thus this scheme starts by collecting "subject-verb" and "verb-object" pairs to see which verbs tend to take what sorts of things as either their subjects or objects. From these one can compute the probability of a particular head noun as the subject or object of a given verb. Furthermore, from these scores one can compute a t-score, much as in [28]. Any probability that did not score at the .10 level (i.e., that had more than a one-in-ten chance of being significantly off) was simply not used in further analysis.

Then the following assumption was made:

$P($relative clause attaches to x | main verb of clause $= v)$

$\quad > P($relative clause attaches to y | main verb of clause $= v)$

$\quad \Leftrightarrow P(x = \text{subject/object} \mid v) > P(y = \text{subject/object} \mid v)$ \hfill (8.14)

where the probabilities are included only if their t-score was significant. If the probabilities for all of the attachments were not significant, then the attachment was left unresolved; if there was at least one significant score, the highest was chosen; if there was a tie, the rightmost attachment was chosen. Unfortunately, because the corpus used for finding the subject/object probabilities was small, the number of insignificant t-scores was large and the majority of cases were left unresolved (see the top line in figure 8.4).

As in Basili et al.'s paper [4], semantic tags were used to overcome this sparse-data problem. Thus, rather than computing the probability of a particular head noun as the subject/object of a verb, Fisher and Riloff computed (see Experiment 2 in figure 8.4) the probability that a noun with a particular semantic tag was the subject/object of a verb. Since there were many fewer semantic tags than head nouns, the counts for the different cases were much larger and thus the t-scores were as well.

Finally, although the amount of training data was small, it was selected so that about half of it was on the topic of terrorism and the other half was general text. The last two lines in figure 8.4 show that the program did much better on the terrorism data, as should be expected, since there was comparatively a large amount of data on a very small topic. (The three head nouns most likely to be the object of "found" in the terrorism data were "body," "weapon," and "corpses.")

8.4   Uniform Use of Lexical/Semantic Information

So far we have looked at proposals for handling two kinds of ambiguity in parsing, and these proposals could be generalized to other kinds of ambiguity as well. Consider the ambiguity in such noun-noun and adjective-noun

	% Correct	% Wrong	% Insignificant
Experiment 1	16.44	.46	83.10
Experiment 2	45.21	6.39	48.40
Exp 2 - Terrorist	55.44	5.43	39.13
Exp 2 - General	37.80	7.09	55.11

Figure 8.4
Results of experiment on relative-clause attachment

combinations as "song bird feeder kit," "metal bird feeder kit," and "novice bird feeder kit." The most reasonable parses for the first two are shown in figure 8.5. Presumably if we collected statistics we would find that "song" modified "bird" more than either "feeder" or "kit," while "metal" had the opposite tendency and "novice" was more likely to modify "kit" than any of the other words (although we would probably have a pretty bad sparse-data problem—a topic to which we will return). Thus here too statistics could be placed in the service of syntactic disambiguation.

It obviously would be desirable to use such information routinely while parsing instead of identifying and solving possibly related problems one at a time. We alluded briefly to such an approach in chapter 5, although there our concern was finding a better language model. In particular, we remarked that in a sentence like "Joe watered his mother's small garden," "garden" would have a higher probability as the direct object of "to water" than simply as the word following "mother's small," as in a trigram model. Thus we suggested routinely parsing a sentence and then conditioning the words on the parse. To put it another way, we said that parsing could help in assigning probabilities to words. In the current chapter we are making the opposite point, the words can help in assigning probabilities to parses (and thus making the intended parse the one assigned the highest probability). The model for both improvements is, however, the same, and that is what we turn to next.

While nobody has yet created such a system, it is not too difficult to imagine what some appropriate equations might look like. To create a language model based upon these ideas, let $s_{1,m}$ be a sequence of m sentences and let $t_{1,m}$ vary over all possible syntactic trees for these sentences:

$$P(s_{1,m}) = \sum_{t_{1,m}} P(s_{1,m}, t_{1,m}) \tag{8.15}$$

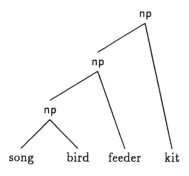 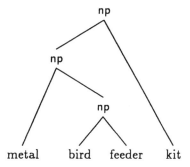

Figure 8.5
Parses of "song/metal bird feeder kit"

$$= \sum_{t_{1,m}} P(t_{1,m}) P(s_{1,m} \mid t_{1,m}) \tag{8.16}$$

$$= \prod_{j=1}^{m} \sum_{t_j} P(t_j) P(s_j \mid t_j) \tag{8.17}$$

Going from equation 8.16 to equation 8.17 requires the usual assumption that the probabilities of the individual sentences are independent of one another. In these equations we assume that the trees t_j go down only to the parts of speech, not the words. (If the trees include the words, then conditioning on them would include conditioning on the words and $P(s_j \mid t_j)$ would be 1.) Here t_j varies over all the parses for s_j and so $P(t_j)$ is just the probability assigned by, say, our PCFG to the particular tree in question. As such we already know how to compute it.

Thus the problematic term in equation 8.17 is $P(s_j \mid t_j)$. Naturally we need to make a few Markov assumptions to turn it into something we can compute. One assumption, this one better than most, is the one we made earlier in this chapter in computing statistics about attachment of prepositional phrases to noun phrases: only the head noun of the noun phrase matters. More generally, for any non-terminal n there is a word w, the head of n, that we can denote $H(n)$. Next, let us give a *breadth- r st numbering* such as that in figure 8.6 to the non-terminals in t_j from the root of the tree down to the parts of speech $(n_1, n_2, \ldots, n_l)$. We can now decompose $P(s_j \mid t_j)$ as follows (where l is the number of non-terminal constituents):

$$P(s_j \mid t_j) = P(H(n_1) \mid t_j) P(H(n_2) \mid t_j, H(n_1)) \ldots$$

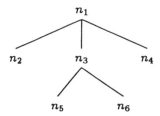

Figure 8.6
Ordering of the non-terminal nodes

$$P(H(n_l) \mid t_j, H(n_1), \ldots, H(n_{l-1})) \tag{8.135}$$

The idea now is to assume that the probability that a word is the head of a given constituent is independent of everything except (1) the word that is the head of its immediate parent and (2) the syntactic relationship between it and its immediate parent. In order to label syntactic relationships, we call $r_{a,b}$ the relationship between the head of the ath rule of the grammar and the bth constituent on its right-hand side. Say the two rules used in producing the tree in figure 8.6 are rules 1 and 2. The syntactic relationships are then as indicated in figure 8.7. We see there that the syntactic relationship between n_1 and n_3 is called $r_{1,2}$ because it is the relation between the head of the first rule and the second element on its right-hand side. Using this notation, we can express our Markov assumption as follows. Let the parent (mother) of n be $M(n)$ and let the syntactic relation between n and $M(n)$ in t_j be $R(n, t_j)$. Then we assume that

$$P(H(n_i) \mid t_j, R(n_i, t_j), H(n_1), \ldots, H(M(n_i)), \ldots, H(n_{i-1}))$$
$$= P(H(n_i) \mid R(n_i, t_j), H(M(n_i)))$$

Using this assumption to simplify equation 8.18, we get

$$P(s_j \mid t_j) = P(H(n_1)) \prod_{i=2}^{l} P(H(n_i) \mid H(M(n_i)), R(n_i, t_j)) \tag{8.136}$$

To make this more concrete, consider the following context-free rules:

r_1 : vp $\rightarrow$ verb np pp

r_2 : np $\rightarrow$ det noun pp

r_3 : pp $\rightarrow$ prep np

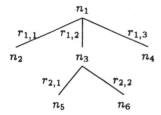

Figure 8.7
Syntactic relations between nodes

Consider $r_{1,2}$, which is the relation between the head of the vp (i.e., the verb) and the head of the np. Thus we would be collecting, and using, the verb-direct-object relationship so useful in this chapter and, as we will see, the next. Or again, consider $r_{1,3}$, and $r_{2,3}$, the relations between the head of a prepositional phrase and the np or vp to which it can attach. Since the head of a prepositional phrase is normally taken to be the preposition, we would be collecting statistics between the attachment point and the preposition and the preposition and the head of the noun phrase within the pp, but we would not be collecting statistics covering all three together. This is roughly parallel to the approach taken by the first of the systems discussed in this chapter.

Despite the rather sweeping nature of our Markov assumption, it is still necessary to reduce drastically the number of parameters required. There are many ways to do this. First, we have been profligate in the number of syntactic relations we consider. For example, our scheme would assign two different relations to the nps in the two rules

vp → verb np

vp → verb np pp

This seems an unnecessary distinction. To a first approximation, if two rules have the same prefix (e.g., verb np in this case) then we can assume that the syntactic relations are the same for the prefix in both rules. There are other ways in which the number of syntactic relations could be reduced as well.

But the major contribution to the number of parameters required is not the number of syntactic relations but the number of lexical items, since we need to collect statistics for each pair of such items. Ultimately, to make the statistics-gathering tractable, words will have to be grouped into clusters with similar distributional properties. This is what the semantic tags of [19] and [4] were intended to do. However, in both of these studies the tags were attached by hand and thus the total number of words tagged was small.

Furthermore, the groupings (tags) themselves were defined for a particular domain, say the legal domain. In general it has proven very difficult to create domain-independent word classes.

The reader should note an implicit assumption here: the tags were *de ned* in terms of their semantics but were to be *used* to predict more "surfacey" phenomena like syntactic disambiguation. Thus we are assuming that words that behave in the same way on the surface have semantic similarities. If this is indeed the case, we might be able to create such groups automatically by collecting statistics on how words behave at the surface level and grouping words with similar statistics. In the next chapter we see that this is indeed a promising approach.

8.5   Exercises

8.1 Equation 8.19 multiplied in the probability of the head of a subcon-stituent, given the head of the constituent and the syntactic relation, for all constituents and subconstituents in the tree. The head of a subconstituent can, however, be the same as the head of the constituent of which it is a part. First, show how this can happen; second, show that equation 8.19 still holds when it does.

8.2 In applying lexical information to syntactic decisions, we needed to give the parts of speech a "breadth-first" numbering. Given a formal characteri-zation of the numbering scheme required.

8.3 In reducing the number of syntactic relations of the form $r_{a,b}$ we said that rules with the same prefix could be collapsed and the syntactic rela-tions as well. First, make up some examples in which this assumption yields reasonable results when applied to the following rules:

np → det adj noun

np → det adj noun pp

np → det adj noun pp wh

(Here wh is a relative clause.) Second, use the following examples to show that for a particular class of verb phrases the prefix assumption fails:

Sue sold the man a car.

Sue sold a car.

9 Word Classes and Meaning

At the end of the previous chapter we sketched a language model in which the statistics were based upon the parses of a sentence. We then considered smoothing the model by collecting statistics not on individual words, but rather on classes of words. At that point, however, there was an interesting division in how we wanted to talk about such classes. First, because the classes were created for use in a language model, they should be useful in predicting subsequent words. But at the same time, it was natural to think of such classes as semantic in nature—certainly the previous work using a class-based approach treated them in this fashion.

This raises an obvious question: if we collect such classes, will they, in fact, show semantic features? In this chapter we answer this question with a tentative "yes."

9.1 Clustering

Grouping words (or anything else) into classes that reflect commonality of some property works as follows:

1. define the properties one cares about, and be able to give numerical values for each property

2. create a vector of length n with the n numerical values for each item to be classified

3. viewing the n-dimensional vector as a point in an n-dimensional space, cluster points that are near one another

This procedure leaves the following points open to variation:

1. the properties used in the vector

2. the distance metric used to decide if two points are "close"

3. the algorithm used to cluster

To take a simple case, suppose we have two properties each ranging between zero and one, and suppose the graph of our data points looks like figure 9.1. Assuming we used the "obvious" distance metric *Euclidean distance*, the distance between points "as the crow flies," then this figure clearly suggests two groups, one with three members, one with four.

Of the three aspects of our clustering procedure that we can vary, it is the first, the properties used, that seems to have the largest effect on the results, and we organize our discussion along this dimension. However, there is no

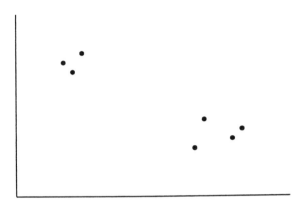

Figure 9.1
A simple clustering problem

doubt a lot of useful work to be done on choosing the proper metric and algorithm for clustering.

9.2 Clustering by Next Word

To take a particular example, in the work reported in Brown et al. [10], each word was characterized by the words that immediately followed it. More formally, $C(x)$ denotes the vector of properties of x (intuitively, x's "context"). In this chapter x is a word type. In the experiment in [10], we can think of our vector for w^i as counts, for each word w^j, of how often w^j followed w^i in the corpus:

$$C(w^i) = \langle\, |\, w^1\, |, |\, w^2\, |, \ldots |\, w^\omega\, |\,\rangle \qquad\qquad (9.137)$$

Now there are many ways to define our distance measure on such vectors. Note that Euclidean distance would not be a good one, as words that occurred often would then be quite distant from rare words, even if they meant pretty much the same thing (and were used in the same way). For example, this would separate "fat" and "obese." Normalizing by the count of w^i would fix this, and then we would have a vector of conditional probabilities $P(w^j \mid w^i)$. However, what Brown et al. did was somewhat different.

To understand their metric we need to introduce a new concept, that of *mutual information*. We first define the mutual information $I(x; y)$ of two particular outcomes x and y as the amount of information one outcome gives us about the other. With the standard idea of information as $-\log P(x)$, this gives us:

$$I(x; y) \overset{\text{def}}{=} (-\log P(x)) - (-\log P(x \mid y)) = \log \frac{P(x, y)}{P(x)P(y)} \qquad (9.2)$$

Suppose we want to to know how much information the word "pancake" gives us about the following word "syrup." The mutual information measure for this would be:

$$I(W_i = \text{pancake}; W_{i+1} = \text{syrup}) = \log \frac{P(W_i = \text{pancake}, W_{i+1} = \text{syrup})}{P(W_i = \text{pancake})P(W_{i+1} = \text{syrup})}$$
$$(9.3)$$

In our usual way, we abbreviate this as

$$I(\text{pancake}; \text{syrup}) = \log \frac{P(\text{pancake}, \text{syrup})}{P(\text{pancake})P(\text{syrup})} \qquad (9.4)$$

A good way to get a feel for this measure is to see how it performs in various limits. For example, if "pancake" and "syrup" have no particular relation to each other then we would expect:

$$P(\text{syrup} \mid \text{pancake}) = P(\text{syrup}) \qquad (9.5)$$

In this case

$$
\begin{aligned}
I(\text{pancake}; \text{syrup}) &= \log \frac{P(\text{pancake}, \text{syrup})}{P(\text{pancake})P(\text{syrup})} \\
&= \log \frac{P(\text{syrup} \mid \text{pancake})}{P(\text{syrup})} \\
&= \log \frac{P(\text{syrup})}{P(\text{syrup})} = 0
\end{aligned}
$$

If they are perfectly coordinated then we get a very large number, as shown by:

$$
\begin{aligned}
I(\text{pancake}; \text{syrup}) &= \log \frac{P(\text{pancake}, \text{syrup})}{P(\text{pancake})P(\text{syrup})} \\
&= \log \frac{P(\text{pancake})}{P(\text{pancake})P(\text{syrup})} \\
&= \log \frac{1}{P(\text{syrup})}
\end{aligned}
$$

It is left as an exercise for the reader to show that if they are negatively correlated the mutual information is a very small negative number.

The *average mutual information* of the random variables X and Y, $I(X; Y)$, is defined as the amount of information we get about X from knowing the value of Y, on the average. Thus its definition is the average over the mutual information of the individual combinations. (We assume that both random variables have possible values $\{w^1, \ldots w^\omega\}$, although we could just as easily assume they have different possible values.)

$$I(X; Y) \stackrel{\text{def}}{=} \sum_{y=1}^{\omega} \sum_{x=1}^{\omega} P(w^x, w^y) I(w^x; w^y) \tag{9.6}$$

Average mutual information can also be formally defined using the notion of conditional entropy (see exercise 9.2).

As we cluster things (words) together, we lose specificity in our predictions and thus the average mutual information decreases. Obviously we would like this decrease to be as small as possible. Thus the metric used in [10] is the minimal loss of average mutual information. Suppose we are considering clustering the words "big" and "large" into a single group. We would first compute $I(W_i; W_{i-1})$ for the separate words. We would then create a class big-large whose vector C(big-large) is derived by summing the individual components of C(big) and C(large). We would then change all the other vectors, e.g., C(the), so that they have $\omega - 1$ components rather than the original ω components (since they lost components for "big" and "large" but gained one for the group). The idea is to find groups in which the loss of mutual information is small. In general, the loss is smaller when the members of the group have similar vectors.

So we have specified what the study in [10] used for $C(w^i)$ and what it used as its distance metric. What remains is the algorithm by which the clusters were created, given this metric. If computational time were no object the algorithm would be trivial. Say we wanted 1000 groups. We would just try all possible groupings into 1000 groups and pick the best on our metric. This is, of course, impossible in real life—there are too many groupings. A typical repair for this problem is to adopt a *greedy algorithm*. In this case this means that the algorithm starts with ω clusters, one for each word. It then combines the two clusters that result in minimal loss of mutual information, and repeats until the desired final number of clusters is reached. This is not guaranteed to find the best clusters, but seems to work well in practice. However, in the study in question, with a vocabulary of 260741 words, even this strategy was too expensive, and instead the algorithm defined 1000 clusters initially, each containing one of the 1000 most common words in the corpus, and then added each of the remaining words to one of these clusters using the greedy method. Some striking clusters are shown in figure 9.2. Note that in several cases the program correctly clustered misspellings with the properly spelled version of the word.

Brown et al. tested these classes in two ways. They built a conventional trigram model and found a per-word cross entropy of 7.93 bits/word. The corresponding model using classes rather than words was measured at 8.08 bits/word: the accuracy has decreased, but the model has considerably fewer parameters. They also used the classes to smooth the trigram model and got a result of 7.88 bits/word. Thus, as one might expect, these classes do capture many of the same regularities as expressed by the trigram model.

In related work Brown et al. [10] clustered words not by the next word, but rather by looking at a window of 1001 words around all tokens of the word in question, excluding the two words on either side. The point here is that combining words with the same lexical environments should group words on the same topic, but removing the two words immediately on either side weakens the grip of syntax. While this could not be used to smooth the kinds of language models we have been proposing, the classes are of interest because at least some of them suggest the beginning of a basis for a knowledge representation. Some examples of the classes they obtained in this way are shown in figure 9.3.

9.3   Clustering with Syntactic Information

Another clustering experiment, this one restricted to nouns, was performed by Pereira and Tishby [36]. They used a partial parser to extract examples of verb-object relations from a corpus, and the context vector for a noun contained the number of times each verb took the noun as its direct object. An example should make this clear. Suppose we have the verbs and nouns shown in figure 9.4. Rather than using actual distributions, we have simply put a "1" if the verb could normally take the noun as its direct object and "0" if doing so would produce an odd sentence (like "Terry timed the mouth"). The associated vector $C(w^i)$ for a word type w^i is the distribution of verbs for which it served as direct object. In our simplified example the contexts for the

Friday Monday Thursday Wednesday Tuesday Saturday Sunday weekends Sundays Saturdays
People guys folks fellows CEOs chaps doubters commies unfortunates blokes
down backwards ashore sideways southward northward overboard aloft downwards adrift
water gas coal liquid acid sand carbon steam shale iron
had hadn't hath would've could've should've must've might've
that tha theat
head body hands eyes voice arm seat eye hair mouth

Figure 9.2
Selected word classes using following-word data

word types "closet," "door," and "meeting" are given by their corresponding rows from figure 9.4:

$$\mathcal{C}(\text{door}) = \langle 1,0,1,1,1,0,0 \rangle$$
$$\mathcal{C}(\text{closet}) = \langle 1,0,1,1,1,0,0 \rangle$$
$$\mathcal{C}(\text{meeting}) = \langle 0,1,0,0,1,1,1 \rangle$$

It should be clear that by this sort of measure "door" and "closet" should look much the same. Indeed, in our example they look *exactly* the same, but real life would also include verbs like "enter," which would make them look slightly different. Nevertheless, they would look much more like each other than either would look like "meeting." Thus distinguishing nouns on the basis of the verbs for which they can serve as direct objects yields a reasonable measure of "semantic distance."

Actually, the vectors for the nouns are not counts of how often each verb had it as object, but rather the probability, given the noun as direct object, that the verb is $v^1, v^2 \dots v^k$. That is,

$$\mathcal{C}(n) = \langle P(v^1 \mid n), P(v^2 \mid n), \dots, P(v^k \mid n) \rangle \tag{9.7}$$

tie jacket suit
attorney counsel trial court judge
letter addressed enclosed letters correspondence
table tables dining chairs plate
published publication author publish writer titled
wall ceiling walls enclosure roof

Figure 9.3
Topically related groups

Nouns	buy	end	wash	touch	Verbs ope1	start	time
conference	0	1	0	0	1	1	1
closet	1	0	1	1	1	0	0
door	1	0	1	1	1	0	0
meeting	0	1	0	0	1	1	1
mouth	0	0	1	1	1	0	0
number	0	0	0	0	0	0	0
reply	0	1	0	0	1	1	1
store	1	0	1	1	1	0	0
window	1	0	1	1	1	0	0

Figure 9.4
Matrix of verbs and their direct objects

The metric used in this study to compare two nouns w^i and w^j is the *relative entropy* of the distributions (as indicated by their vectors) for the two nouns. We do not define relative entropy here. The clustering algorithm is different as well, and again we do not go into details except to note that it starts not with a predefined number of groups but with one group and splits it successively until the desired number of groups are realized. This creates an interesting tree structure of groups, part of which is shown in figure 9.5. The words in each box represent the nouns that are closest to the *centroid* (the most central point) of the cluster. As one moves toward the leaves of the tree, the groups become more clearly semantic in nature.

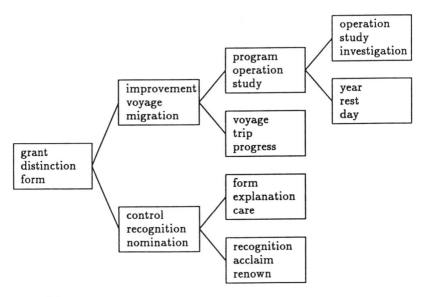

Figure 9.5
Cluster tree for verb-object clustering

Grefenstette [26] tried a similar approach, but characterized nouns by more properties than just the verbs for which they served as object. He applied a partial parsers to find the major syntactic relations in the text. Then he stored all the other words that were related to each noun (in another study [24] he looked at adjectives in much the same way); when subject, object, and indirect-object relations could be distinguished, it noted these as well. So for the sentence "Jack ate a yellow banana" it would find the relations

Jack ate subject   banana ate object   banana yellow

Thus for each noun w^i, $C(w^i)$ is a vector of counts for every other word w^j and each of the four possible syntactic relations between w^i and w^j: subject, object, indirect-object, and "neutral" (as in "yellow banana").

The metric used was a weighted Tanimoto measure [41]. Though again we do not explain this in detail, a binary Tanimoto measure is easy to understand. It is a measure of similarity (so that smaller values indicate increasing distance between concepts) defined as:

$$\frac{|\text{ attributes shared by } x \text{ and } y \,|}{|\text{ unique attributes possessed by } x \text{ or } y \,|} \tag{9.8}$$

So, if "banana" and "apple" had the attributes

banana: yellow, ate object, drop subject, ripe
apple: red, ate object, drop subject

the similarity measure would be 2/5. The weighted version of this metric multiplies each attribute by a weight to reflect the importance of the attribute for that noun.

Unfortunately, Grefenstette [26] did not used his scheme to construct word classes. Instead, he found the most similar word to each noun in his corpus—four million words in the area of medicine. The results for the most common nouns are shown in figure 9.6. Note that the "closest" relation need not be symmetric: while "case" is closest to "patient" and vice versa, this is not true for "study" and "change."

It is interesting to ask whether any technique presented in this section does a better job than others in creating groups with semantic regularities. The only study we know on this issue is that of Grefenstette [25]. He compares his syntactically based scheme to a window scheme (like that of Brown et al. [10]). He used a ten-word window, not going over sentence boundaries and only using nouns, adjectives, and verbs found in the window; as his "gold standard" for semantic similarity he used Roget's Thesaurus [1]. He then employed the following measurement:

Given a corpus, use the similarity extraction method to derive similarity judgments between the words appearing in the corpus. For each word, take the word appearing as most similar. Examine the human compiled thesaurus to see if that pair of words appears under the same topic number. If it does, count this as a hit [25].

He found that, for the approximately 2700 nouns appearing ten or more times in his four-million-word corpus, the syntactic method gave more hits for 300 most common words and the window method did better for the rest. (For example, on the most common 20 nouns the window method gave 30% hits, while the syntactic method gave 50% hits.) It seems likely that this result is due principally to sparse-data problems for the syntactic method when the words have comparatively low frequency—the window method provides many more data points for each word token than the syntactic method. One would thus expect that, as the methods are applied to larger corpora, the area over which the syntactic method is superior will increase.

While the above seems to argue in favor of the syntactic method, one aspect of the test is not quite fair to the window method. In a very interesting

Word	Closest	Word	Closest
cell	tissue	case	patient
patient	case	level	concentration
effect	response	result	effect
study	change	response	effect
change	increase	child	patient

Figure 9.6
Most similar nouns using syntactic relations

experiment, Gale et al. [22] have shown that useful information about words can be as far as 1000 words away. This suggests that Grefenstette's ten-word window may be too narrow and that window method might acquit itself better with a much larger window size. (See section 10.1 for more on the Gale et al. experiment.)

9.4   Problems with Word Clustering

While the results achieved by these word-grouping techniques are indeed impressive, we have given an over-rosy impression by concentrating on their successes at the expense of cases where they did not do as well. There are several reasons why these techniques may not produce classes with semantic coherence. First and foremost, for low-frequency words the data obtained from the few examples may be quite unrepresentative. In many of the studies low-frequency words were simply removed. However, Grefenstette [26] gives the following low-frequency nouns with their closest word:

breast—undergoing   childhood—psychosis   outflow—infundibulum

Other low-frequency words, however, came out fine.

Next, there are limits on the kind of distinctions that such surface phenomena can make. For example, Grefenstette's study [24] for adjectives similar to the one mentioned earlier found that the most similar adjectives according to his measure were typical antonyms. Figure 9.7 shows word/most-similar-word pairs for the most common adjectives in his corpus. Note that not all of them are antonyms: the pair "shallow-coastal" is more like a synonym. That antonyms can come out most similar, however, shows that there are some

Word	Most similar	Word	Most similar
large	small	short	long
small	large	strong	weak
new	major	black	white
high	low	heavy	light
long	short	white	black
low	high	shallow	coastal

Figure 9.7
Adjectives and their most similar adjectives

possibly intrinsic limits to how finely we can group semantically simply by looking at surface phenomena.

In addition, these techniques can sometimes produce strange results for reasons that are not immediately apparent. Figure 9.8 gives some sobering examples.

Lastly, the source of one problem is all too apparent. One run of the next-word-grouping experiment found the class

January February March April June July August September October November December

Do you know what the problem is? As a hint, consider that in the adjective experiment the word most similar to "right" was indeed, "left," but only by a little bit; the second-most-similar word was "privilege."

9.5 Exercises

9.1 Most of the context vectors $C(w^j)$ have an entry for w^j itself. Is this reasonable? Discuss.

9.2 In this exercise we derive equation 9.6 from more general principles. First, let us formally define the notion of *conditional entropy* $H(X \mid Y)$ of the random variables X given the random variable Y:

$$H(X \mid Y) = -\sum_{y=1}^{\omega} \sum_{x=1}^{\omega} P(w^y) P(w^x \mid w^y) \log P(w^x \mid w^y) \tag{9.9}$$

Method	Clinkers
Grouping by direct object	state people modern
	pollution increase failure
Groupings by next word	industry producers makers fishery Arabia growers addiction medalist inhalation addict
	little prima moment's trifle tad Litle minute's tinker's hornet's teammate's
Adjective comparison	full-increase
	bottom-zone
	sweet-anticlimatic

Figure 9.8
Some not-so-semantic groupings

Next, define average mutual information as follows:

$$I(X;Y) = H(X) - H(X \mid Y) \tag{9.10}$$

Show that this definition implies equation 9.6.

9.3 Implement an efficient algorithm to find the next word to cluster using the metric of minimal loss of mutual information. This algorithm should take into account that (a) we never need to know the actual mutual information, just the change due to combining two clusters, and (b) combining two clusters leaves most aspects of the mutual information unchanged.

9.4 There are many metrics for measuring distance between context vectors, and many clustering algorithms. Very little is known about how much the clusters one gets depends on either of these factors. So, for example, rather than using the measure of minimal loss of mutual information, suppose one used Euclidean distance on the conditional probabilities of the next word in the text after the occurrences of a given word type. How do the clusters look? Use the clusters in place of words in a trigram model. Does the metric make much difference in how well the clusters work? Do the same for using them to smooth a language model.

10 Word Senses and Their Disambiguation

A word that has more than one meaning (or *word sense*) is called *polysemous*. In this chapter we ask first how to identify polysemous words using statistical information, and second how to use statistical information to discover the intended sense of a polysemous word from context.

Our approach here is in many respects like that in the previous chapter. To discover polysemy we create vectors—points in n-dimensional space—and cluster them. However, where in chapter 9 the points were word types and the clusters were semantic classes, here each point is a word token and the clusters are word senses. The idea is that any use of a polysemous word (where the use itself corresponds to a word token) has a context and that the contexts associated with uses of the word will clump together into distinct groups according to the intended sense of the word token.

To be more concrete, suppose we collect statistical information on each occurrence of "bank" in our corpus. When we graph this we would expect to get something like figure 9.1 in chapter 9, where each dot gives the context of a token of the word "bank" and the clusters would represent, we hope, the word senses savings-institution and river-edge. Now suppose we find a new occurrence of "bank" and want to know its intended meaning. Obviously we look at the cluster it belongs to. Thus the techniques of this chapter start out much like those of the last:

1. specify the contextual properties in numerical terms

2. for each token to be classified, create a vector of length n with the n numerical values for that token

3. viewing the n-dimensional vector as a point in an n-dimensional space, cluster points that are near each other

To these, however, we need to add two further steps:

4. summarize the information about the properties of each cluster

5. define a procedure that, given a new token, uses the cluster information from (4) to decide the intended meaning.

10.1 Word Senses Using Outside Information

One way to cluster vectors into groups is to have information telling you which vectors belong to which group. For example, it could tell you that a particular token of "bank" is either the river-edge sense or the savings-institution sense. Work by Gale et al. [22] and Brown et al. [9] used a large corpus of parallel English and French taken from the proceedings of the Canadian parliament (called the "Hansards"). Anybody who has looked into machine translation (using computers to translate from a "source" language to a "target" language) is aware that word-sense ambiguity is a problem because one word in the source language can have different translations in the target language. Often this is because the source word has more than one meaning. Conversely, however, we could use a translation to get an indication of the intended meaning of the source word.

For example, the word "duty" in English has two senses, a kind of tax and an obligation. No single word in French has this same ambiguity. Rather, most of the time "duty" translates as either "droit" (the tax) or "devoir" (the obligation). There are now techniques for aligning parallel French-English corpora and thereby finding the French translation of a particular word (or vice versa) assuming that the translation is a single word (as it is in this case) (see [8]). Thus if we restrict consideration to cases where the French translation is either "droit" or "devoir," we have an automatic classification of the English context into one of the two senses of "duty." Note also that we can get counts of how often each sense appears and thus can estimate $P(\text{tax})$ and $P(\text{obligation})$. Figure 10.1 gives five ambiguous English words and the French for two of their senses, and shows how often each sense was found in the parallel English-French corpus. This figure and the rest of our description are taken from Gale et al. [22], as the approach used there fits better into our presentation than does that of Brown et al. [9]. The results obtained in both are quite similar.

Let us start from the beginning of Gale et al.'s "procedure" for word-sense disambiguation. The first step is to define the context vector for word tokens. In this study it is the number of occurrences of each word type in a 100-word window around the token in question:

$$C(w_i) = \left\langle \mid w^1 \mid, \mid w^2 \mid, \ldots, \mid w^{\omega} \mid \right\rangle \tag{10.1}$$

Here $\mid w^j \mid$ is the number of times the word type w^j appears in the 100-word window around the word token w_i. The program then uses the translation information to classify each such point, and the classified vectors are used formally to define the prototype word-sense contexts. In particular, all of

English	French	Sense	Number of examples
duty	droit	tax	1114
	devoir	obligation	691
drug	médicament	medical	2292
	drogue	illicit	855
land	terre	property	1022
	pays	country	386
position	position	place	5177
	poste	job	577
sentence	peine	judicial	296
	phrase	grammatical	148

Figure 10.1
Ambiguities resolved via French translation

the vectors for, say, the "tax" sense of "duty" are combined to define the following vectors:

$$C(\text{tax}) = \langle P(w^1 \mid \text{tax}), \cdots, P(w^\omega \mid \text{tax}) \rangle \tag{10.2}$$

where $P(w^i \mid \text{tax})$ is the probability that one of the words in the window around an occurrence of the "tax" sense of "duty" is w^i. Then given a new example of "duty," w_i, for which we do not have the French translation, we can decide on the word's intended sense using the following equation, where s varies over the senses of the word in question:

$$\arg\max_s P(s \mid C(w_i)) = \arg\max_s \frac{P(s)P(C(w_i) \mid s)}{P(C(w_i))} \tag{10.3}$$

$$= \arg\max_s P(s)P(C(w_i) \mid s) \tag{10.4}$$

$$= \arg\max_s P(s) \prod_{x \in C(w_i)} P(x \mid s) \tag{10.5}$$

Here the first two equations are exact while the last assumes that in a given context s the words that appear around it are independent of one another—not a great assumption, but probably fine for this application. We have already seen how to get the quantities required by equation 10.5: we calculate $P(s)$ by noting how many times each French translation is used, while the various $P(x \mid s)$ are just the quantities used in the definition of the sense contexts of equation 10.2.

A particularly serious problem with this approach is the possibility that some $P(x \mid s)$ of equation 10.5 are wildly off because of sparse data. The most obvious case is when a $P(x \mid s)$ is zero because it just so happened that in all the training cases the word x was never in the window around an instance of s. The result would be that the critical quantity in equation 10.5 would be zero, no matter how likely the other words in the 100-word window were, given the sense. To guard against this case, Gale et al. smooth the $P(x \mid s)$ with the prior probabilities for the word, $P(x)$, so as to prevent such unseemly zeros.

Gale et al. report that over all of the ambiguous words of figure 10.1 they get a 10% error rate. They do not break down this result by individual words, although they give a lot of other interesting information. For example, in one experiment they replaced the 100-word window by a 10-word window at various distances from the word they were trying to disambiguate. They found that a 10-word window as far away as 1000 words from the test word still improved the disambiguation decision to a better-than-chance level. Further away than that the decision went down to chance level.

Another interesting experiment in which sense classification was done using a second source of information is described by Yarowsky [44]. He assumed that each sense of a word corresponded to one and only one of the 1042 classes of words treated in Roget's International Thesaurus [1]. For example, the English word "crane" has two senses, one corresponding to the Roget class tool and the other to animal. Yarowsky first gathers statistics for each Roget class, exactly as Gale et al. do for equation 10.2, but the probability is taken not with respect to a word sense like "tax" but with respect to a Roget class, e.g., tool. For example, for the class animal we would find all corpus occurrences of any of the words in the class (e.g., species, family, bird, fish, breed, etc.) and get their 100-word windows; the words appearing in these windows would become counts for equation 10.2. Again, the prior probabilities of words were included to smooth the counts. Given these statistics, a decision is made on a new test case using equation 10.5. Yarowsky reports results on 12 words, with from two to six senses (the average is slightly above three); some of these are given in figure 10.2.

10.2 Word Senses Without Outside Information

Next we consider an experiment by Schütze [39,40] that is similar to that of Gale et al. in using word counts from a 100-word window. In this work, however, there is no source of outside information to help select the sense being used, and the context vectors are slightly different as well.

The impetus for this second change is our ever-present sparse data problem. It can often happen that few of the words surrounding any instance of a content word are, in fact, really related to it in any direct way. To make this more concrete, the author performed the following informal experiment. In a book I was reading on the political history of the space race, I picked two points in the book "at random" and scanned forward for the first occurrence of the word "space." The idea was that these contexts might be used to distinguish the meaning of "space" as "the region beyond the earth's atmosphere" from a meaning such as "a boundless three-dimensional extent in which objects move" (though given the book's subject I anticipated finding only the former). Here are the two contexts found, where we used just a 50-word window to keep things short.

that program ..." Hence the line to be adopted at the UN against Soviet verbal assaults: the United States would admit to having military programs in *space*, but stress their importance to peace and contrast American candor to Soviet secrecy. Even liberal Senator Albert Gore (D., Tenn.) concurred: "no workable dividing line ([33], p. 348)

of the world, then the United States must show that its affluence reached the poor and colored at home. Rostow also had strong views on *space* policy. As a member of the Greenewalt Committee, he considered technological competition to be critical and had "a bias toward hope rather than skepticism." But ([33], p. 217)

We then informally picked out words that could more or less be considered content words. The alphabetized lists for the two contexts are shown side by side in figure 10.3. The significant point here is the relative lack of overlap between the word groups. Indeed, of all the content words we picked, only "United" and "States" appeared in both contexts. These words are rather slim pickings on which to base a decision that these two contexts are similar in selecting the "outer space" meaning of "space." (From the work of Gale et al.

Word	Sense	Roget category	N	% Correct
star	space object	universe	1422	96
	celebrity	entertainer	222	95
	star-shaped object	insignia	56	82
mole	quantity	chemicals	95	98
	mammal	animal	46	100
	skin blemish	disease	13	100
	digging machine	support	4	100
slug	animal	animal	24	100
	type strip	printing	8	100
	mass unit	weight	3	100
	fake coin	money	2	50
	metallurgy	impact	1	100
	bullet	arms	1	100

Figure 10.2
Ambiguities and Roget classes

[22], it would seem that this problem may not be too bad, since the method as reported there seems to perform quite well. However, the problem may be worse for Schütze's approach as he does not have an outside source of information.) At any rate, there are other words in our "space" example, not shared, that would seem useful in such a disambiguation, such as "military," "program," "policy," and "technological." To give such words a larger role, Schütze uses as "context" not the neighboring words, but rather the words that the neighboring words normally consort with. For each word type w^i we define an associated vector $A(w^i)$, the average context of word type w^i. That is, let c_k^j be the number of times w^j appears within 100 words of word token w_k. Then the associated vector (average context) of w^i is given by

$$A(w^i) = \sum_{k=1}^{n} \delta(i,k) \left\langle c_k^1, c_k^2, \ldots, c_k^\omega \right\rangle \qquad (10.6)$$

Page 348	Page 217	Page 348	Page 217
adopted	affluence	military	policy
Albert		peace	poor
American		program	rather
admit		secrecy	reached
assaults	bias	Senator	Rostow
candor	colored	Soviet	skepticism
concurred	Committee	States	States
contrast	competition	stress	strong
D.	considered	Tenn.	technological
dividing	critical	UN	
Gore	Greenewalt	United	United
importance	home	verbal	views
liberal	hope	workable	world
line	member		

Figure 10.3
Significant words in two contexts for "space"

Here n is the number of words in our training text and $\delta(i, k)$, which simply picks out the contexts of w^i, is defined as:

$$\delta(i, k) = \begin{cases} 1 & \text{if } w_k = w^i \\ 0 & \text{otherwise} \end{cases} \tag{10.7}$$

Naturally the sum of vectors is taken in the usual way, by adding the individual components separately. From this we compute the context of a word token w_j as follows:

$$C(w_j) = \sum_{i=1}^{\omega} c_j^i A(w^i) \tag{10.8}$$

The idea is that while the words "military," "program," "policy," and "technological" do not appear in both contexts, the words they themselves have appeared next to overlap significantly.

Perhaps an (invented) example will help. Suppose two tokens of "bank" have no significant words in common, but one has the word "money" nearby and the other has the word "loan." Furthermore, suppose we have the following contexts for these two word types (we throw in "water" for comparison):

	bank	building	loan	money	mortgage	river	water
loan	150	20	70	100	50	10	40
money	600	500	100	400	50	30	70
water	50	400	40	70	1	400	500

There are several things to note here. First, although the vectors for "loan" and "money" we have created are not all that similar, they at least give more overlap than we had from the direct contexts (which was no overlap at all). Second, in making up these numbers we assumed that the words "money" and "water" are much more common than "loan" and thus would have many more context words. Thus much of the difference between "loan" and "money" is simply due to the vector length. But obviously when looking at context we are interested in the overall pattern of usage, not the absolute numbers. Thus it would make sense to use a similarity measure other than Euclidean distance, as the latter is quite sensitive to vector length. Schütze's similarity measure is the cosine of the angle between the two vectors, which is independent of the vector lengths but should be related to the overall distribution. The cosine of the angle between two m-dimensional vectors $\vec{a}$ and $\vec{b}$ is given by

$$\cos(\vec{a}, \vec{b}) = \frac{\sum_{k=1}^{m} a_k b_k}{\sqrt{\left(\sum_{k=1}^{m} (a_k)^2\right)\left(\sum_{k=1}^{m}(b_k)^2\right)}} \tag{10.9}$$

The maximum value (one) occurs when the cosine is of two vectors pointing in the same direction. As defined here, the minimum cosine is zero, and this occurs when one of the vectors has a zero in every place where the other is nonzero. In the cases at hand, we find that cos(loan, money) = .838, as compared, for example, to cos(loan, water) = .316. Of course, in a real example we do not know a priori which words to pull out as important, and thus we take the average over all of the words. This dilutes the effect, but the principle remains that we smooth the statistics by considering not just the nearby words, but their contexts as well.

Figure 10.4 shows the results obtained in [39,40]. The first two columns give the number of examples used first to train and then to test. The next

Word	Number of examples		Number of classes	% rare	% major	% correct
	training	test				
tank/s	1780	336	8	16	80	95
plant/s	4132	502	13	14	66	92
interest/s	2955	501	3	15	68	93
capital/s	2000	200	2	5	66	95
suit/s	8206	498	2	18	54	95
motion/s	3101	200	2	0	54	92
ruling	5966	200	2	4	60	90
vessel/s	1701	144	7	10	58	92
space	10126	200	10	0	59	90
train/s	4775	266	10	2	76	89

Figure 10.4
Ten disambiguation experiments

three columns indicate the number of classes (senses) into which the word was divided, the percentage of training tokens judged to be in none of these classes, and the percentage of the total comprised by the most common sense. (This last indicates how well the "dumb" algorithm "pick the most common sense" would perform.) The final column indicates how well the program did at assigning senses to the test data.

This scheme has other interesting aspects. We have not said how the contexts were classified (some were classified using AutoClass [14], and some using Buckshot [17]). The amount of data this method requires is also an issue. If we assume there are, say, 50,000 words and 100,000 senses, then every sense should have associated with it a vector of length 50,000 and the total space requirement is $5 \cdot 10^9$. (The same is true for the work of Gale et al.) This is rather steep. Schütze has experimented with data-reduction methods, which we do not discuss here.

10.3 Meanings and Selectional Restrictions

In the previous section we considered how to use the surrounding words to distinguish different contexts. A second possibility (though they are hardly mutually exclusive) is to consider in more detail the context created by the sentence in which the word token appears. Obviously, if we treat the sentence as an unordered set of words, this would differ little from what we did in the last section. However, suppose we can parse the sentence and establish relations between the words. That is, suppose that in the sentence "The dog ate the green apples" we know that "the dog" is the subject of the sentence, that "the green apples" is the direct object, and that within this direct object "apples" is the head noun and is modified by "green." Such information can be much more useful than an unordered set of nearby words. For example, consider the sentences "Susan opened the meeting" and "Susan opened the door." In deciding whether or not "open" has different senses in the two sentences, the fact that it appears near the word "meeting" in one and "door" in the other gives some weak evidence. But the fact that "meeting" and "door" appear as the direct object of "open" is much stronger evidence that there are two senses here.

It is worth making our chain of reasoning more explicit here. Most verbs denote some action. As noted in chapter 1, verbs put selectional restrictions on the kinds of things that can fill certain roles in a sentence. Presumably verbs differ in their selectional restrictions because the different actions they denote are normally performed with different objects. Thus we can distinguish word senses by distinguishing selectional restrictions. Of course, learning the selectional restrictions for verbs is worthwhile in its own right.

There is, however, one major problem in all of this. Figure 10.5 gives a list of direct objects for the verb "open" (from [37]). We have informally classified the objects into two groups: (1) physical objects with interiors and portals thereof, and (2) times and events that can start. More fine-grained classifications are possible. However, in terms of any statistical procedure, this is simply a list of words: there is no more reason, at least so far, to group "church" with "store" than with "reply." And, of course, we have the typical sparse-data problem. Lots of other things can be opened, such as "cans," "hatches," and "lectures," to name only a few. How can these words be included in the list without letting in other words that we would normally classify as unopenable, such as "number" and "emotion"?

One possible solution is to use outside information in order to recognize the implicit groups. Thus Resnik in [37] uses a system called WordNet [34] that among other things includes a hierarchy of word groups. The idea is to see which predefined group or groups have the best "fit" with the observed words.

Object	Count	Object	Count
door	26	closet	2
mouth	7	window	5
church	2	store	2
eye	7		
season	2	scene	3
statement	2	chapter	2
time	2	minute	2
discourse	1	engagement	1
reply	1	program	1
conference	1	session	1

Figure 10.5
Words appearing as the direct object of "open"

The measure used for fit is a variant of the mutual information measure introduced in section 9.2. In [37], the mutual information of a verb v and a class of nouns c, $I(v; c)$, is the probability of the verb taking any noun in the class as its direct object divided by the product of the probability of v and the probability of any member of c being the direct object of any verb:

$$I(v; c) = \log \frac{P(v, c)}{P(v)P(c)} \tag{10.10}$$

One drawback of the mutual-information measure for this task is that in general it prefers very small classes, since it is usually easier to get a small class to fit a verb than a larger one. The following measure was used in this study to counteract this tendency;

$$A(v, c) \stackrel{\text{def}}{=} P(c \mid v)I(v; c) \tag{10.11}$$

The first term is generally larger for larger classes, since as the class c grows the more likely the direct object of a verb is to be in it. That this approach can work is suggested by figure 10.6 (from [37]), which shows some verbs, the WordNet class with the highest $A(v, c)$ value, and the value of $A(v, c)$ obtained.

Verb	Object class	$A(v,c)$	Verb	Object class	$A(v,c)$
call	someone	.16	ignore	question	.81
catch	looking_at	.30	mix	intoxicant	2.29
climb	stair	2.39	move	article_of_commerce	.26
close	movable_barrier	1.15	need	helping	.39
cook	repast	3.64	stop	vehicle	.66
draw	cord	.27	take	spatial_property	.34
eat	nutrient	1.76	work	change_of_place	.45
forget	conception	.45			

Figure 10.6
Object classes for the direct objects of some verbs

One problem that may be endemic but is most clear with this program is a tendency to "overfit" the data. For example, the topmost class for "open" is door. Thus topmost classes by themselves do not do the job, and one must go down to secondary classes. Those for "open," besides door, are entrance, mouth, repository, container, time_period, oral_communication, and writing. (This may also be true for Schütze's work [39,40]: note in figure 10.4 the number of senses for "plant" (13), "space" (10), and "train" (10).)

A second approach to finding selectional restrictions of verbs is suggested in the work of Pereira and Tishby [36]. We saw in section 9.3 how to use the information they collected on verb-direct object combinations to classify nouns by the vectors of verbs that take them as objects. This information can also be used to detect word-sense ambiguity in verbs, since it is reflected in the direct objects they take. In particular, the vectors for each noun can, in effect, solve the problem Resnik had—that the list of direct objects in itself had no structure. Pereira and Tishby can use the noun-context vectors to reveal structure.

Consider again the verb-object table in figure 9.4, this time concentrating on the nouns that are the direct objects of "open." We observe that "open" has two types of direct objects, one resembling "door" and one resembling "meeting":

$\mathcal{C}(\text{door}) = \langle 1,0,1,1,1,0,0 \rangle$

$\mathcal{C}(\text{meeting}) = \langle 0,1,0,0,1,1,1 \rangle$

These can be formalized by, say, taking the centroid of the vectors for each case. Furthermore, suppose that, while our corpus did not actually have an instance of "open a store," comparison of the vector for "store" to the centroid vectors for the two kinds of direct objects shows it is similar to that for "door." Thus we would be able to accept "store" as a reasonable direct object for "open" and assign to "open" its correct sense, despite the fact that "store" had never appeared before as its direct object. Contrast this with "number." If asked whether it would be a reasonable direct object for "open," we would answer no: its vector, $\langle 0,0,0,0,0,0,0 \rangle$, looks nothing like either of the two centroid vectors for this verb.

Pereira and Tishby report on only one disambiguation experiment, on classifying the direct objects of the verb "to fire." As noted in section 9.4, their clustering method (a maximum-entropy approach [38]) breaks down the data into successively finer divisions, thus giving a hierarchy of clusters. The clusters found for the objects of "fire" are shown in figure 10.7: the program first finds the two major meanings of "to fire" and then is able to distinguish to some degree between firing a bullet and firing a gun.

Pereira and Tishby remark that this technique could be used to disambiguate nouns as well. Here, rather than characterizing a noun as a vector of verbs, one would characterize a verb as a vector of nouns. For example, suppose we want to distinguish two senses of the noun "plant." Consider the verbs "cut," "build," "grow," and "paint." Looking at their direct objects might give us a matrix like that in figure 10.8. We now get context vectors for the verb types, and we see that the verbs that can apply to "plant" have two clusters of vectors, one like "grow" and one like "build," suggesting that there are two meanings for this noun. Then, just as in the inverse case, should we see "plant" used as a direct object of a new verb, say "to water," we would look at the vector for this verb and see that it looks more like "grow" than "build," thus suggesting the correct sense for "plant."

10.4   Discussion

We said at the outset of this text that we wanted to use outside information only when absolutely necessary. Thus, among the techniques we have seen for word-sense discovery and disambiguation, our preference leans toward the 100-word-window and the verb-direct-object schemes. Of these two we further suspect that the latter is generally more sensitive, but this is just a guess. The disadvantage of the direct-object scheme, and more generally of

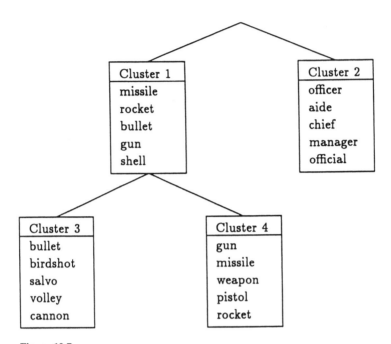

Figure 10.7
Direct objects of "to fire"

classifications based on any syntactic relation, is that it assumes we can get
the required parsing information. But syntactic parsing seems worth doing
for other reasons, and there is no reason not to exploit the extra information
it provides. It would also be possible to combine the parsing and 100-word-
window schemes. It would be interesting to find out if their combination
works better than either by itself.

In this chapter we have made the classical assumptions that each word type
has a small number of distinct senses and that each word token in the corpus
can and should be assigned to exactly one of them. Many have problems
with this assumption. For example, in our discussion of the verb "open" we
distinguished between things that are or have openings and things that are
times or events. Immediately we could ask if we should distinguish four
meanings for "open," one each for portals, things that have portals, times,
and events. Nor need we stop there. Does "open an eye" have the same
meaning of "open" as "open a box"? What about "open one's mouth"? Is

	factory	flower	house	plant	tree
cut	0	1	0	1	1
build	1	0	1	1	0
grow	0	1	0	1	1
paint	1	0	1	1	0

Figure 10.8
Another matrix of verbs and their direct objects

there a reason to make a sharp distinction between them? Schütze makes a similar point with the following example from *The New York Times:*

In Texas, Williams, a millionaire businessman with interests in oil, cattle and banking, was hurt among voters who considered ethics an important issue.

The question is, does "interests" refer to "economic share" or "special attention"? Perhaps it refers to both.

In situations like this it pays to keep in mind the task we want to perform and ask how an assumption like distinct word senses helps or hinders its accomplishment. Consider our prototype task of predicting the next word. It would seem that once we have correlated verbs, say, with context vectors on the basis of the direct objects normally associated with them, assigning a specific meaning to the verb is not necessary.

This is correct, but there is a little more to the story. In particular, we suggested at the end of chapter 8 that word classes might be a way to smooth language models, particularly syntactically based models. Then at the end of chapter 9 we noted that words with more than one sense are a problem in creating such classes, since a single word may well deserve to belong to more than one class. This is most obvious when a word belongs to more than one part of speech, e.g., "may" or "can." However, if the classes are fine enough, more traditional word-sense ambiguity can causes this as well, e.g., "fire" as a verb. The natural solution to this problem is to put such words in more than one class. But this is remarkably close to the classical assumptions, except that the number of classes to which a word belongs replaces the number of senses it is deemed to have.

Fortunately, we do not have to decide on such matters here. The statistical approach we advocate is neutral on this topic, and the status of such standard assumptions can and should change as we learn more about applying the methodology to the problems, and more about the problems as well.

10.5 Exercises

10.1 In our discussion of the cosine measure for the similarity of two vectors we noted that by our definition the minimum value of the measure would be zero. Of course, the minimum cosine is normally -1. Explain this difference. What possibly useful redefinition of our vectors would allow negative cosine values?

10.2 For each of the following nouns, add a row in figure 9.4: "burrow," "conversation," "cup," "lid," and "painting." On the basis of the context vectors just created: (1) would the vectors predict the correct answer to the question, "Is this the sort of thing that can be opened?" (2) if the answer is yes, would the vector correctly characterize the meaning of "open" when applied to this noun? In each case justify your answer or, if the case is not completely clear, explain why.

10.3 Suppose we added the verbs "to shout" and "to splinter" to figure 9.4. Would they tend to make decisions on the meaning of "open" crisper or more fuzzy, or would the change differ for different decisions? Explain your answers.

10.4 We noted that most of the disambiguation work based upon 100-word windows require large amounts of space to store the resulting vectors. Explain why the method based upon Roget categories requires less space than the others.

Bibliography

[1] *Roget's International Thesaurus—Fourth Edition.* Chapman, 1977.

[2] Angluin, D. Queries and concept learning. *Machine Learning 2* (1988), 319–342.

[3] Angluin, D., and Smith, C. H. Inductive inference: theory and methods. *Computing Surveys 15* 3 (1983), 237–269.

[4] Basili, R., Pazienza, M. T., and Velardi, P. *Combining NLP and statistical techniques for lexical acquisition.* In *Working Notes, Fall Symposium Series.* AAAI, 1992, 1–9.

[5] Baum, L. E. An inequality and associated maximization technique in statistical estimation for probabilistic functions of a Markov process. *Inequalities 3* (1972), 1–8.

[6] Boggess, L., Agarwal, R., and Davis, R. *Disambiguation of prepositional phrases in automatically labeled technical text.* In *Proceedings of the Ninth National Conference on Arti cial Intelligence.* AAAI Press/MIT Press, Menlo Park, 1991, 155–159

[7] Briscoe, T., and Waegner, N. *Robust stochastic parsing using the inside-ouside algorithm.* In *Workshop Notes, Statistically-Based NLP Techniques.* AAAI, 1992, 30–53.

[8] Brown, P., Lai, J., and Mercer, R. *Aligning sentences in parallel corpora.* In *Proceedings of the Association for Computational Linguistics.* ACL, 1991, 169–176.

[9] Brown, P. F., Pietra, S. A. D., Pietra, V. J. D., and Mercer, R. L. *Word-sense disambiguation using statistical methods.* In *Proceedings of Association for Computational Linguistics.* ACL, 1991, 264–270.

[10] Brown, P. F., Pietra, V. J. D., DeSouza, P. V., Lai, J. C., and Mercer, R. L. Class-based n-gram models of natural language. *Computational Linguistics 18* 4 (1992), 467–479.

[11] Carroll, G., and Charniak, E. *Two experiments on learning probabilistic dependency grammars from corpora.* In *Workshop Notes, Statistically-Based NLP Techniques.* AAAI, 1–13.

[12] Carroll, G., and Charniak, E. *Learning probabilistic dependency grammars from labeled text.* In *Working Notes, Fall Symposium Series.* AAAI, 1992, 25–32.

[13] Charniak, E., Hendrickson, C., Jacobson, N., and Perkowitz, M. *Equations for part-of-speech tagging.* In *Proceedings of the Eleventh National Conference on Arti cial Intelligence.* AAAI Press/MIT Press, Menlo Park, 1993.

[14] Cheesman, P., Kelly, J., Self, M., Stutz, J., Taylor, W., and Freeman, D. *AutoClass: a Bayesian classi cation system.* In *Proceedings of the Fifth International Conference on Machine Learning.* Morgan Kaufmann, San Mateo, CA, 1988, 54–64.

[15] Chomsky, N. *Lectures on Government and Binding.* Foris Publications, Dordrecht, Holland, 1981.

[16] Church, K. W. *A stochastic parts program and noun phrase parser for unrestricted text.* In *Second Conference on Applied Natural Language Processing.* ACL, 1988, 136–143.

[17] Cutting, D., Karger, D., Pedersen, J., and Tukey, J. *Scatter-gather: a cluster-based approach to browsing large document collections.* In *SIGIR'92.* ACM, New York, 1992.

[18] DeRose, S. J. Grammatical category disambiguation by statistical optimization. *Computational Linguistics 14* (1988), 31–39.

[19] Fisher, D., and Riloff, E. *Applying statistical methods to small corpora: bene ting from a limited domain.* In *Working Notes, Fall Symposium Series.* AAAI, 1992, 47–53.

[20] Francis, W. N., and Kučera, H. *Frequency Analysis of English Usage: Lexicon and Grammar.* Houghton Mifflin, Boston, 1982.

[21] Fu, K. S., and Booth, T. L. Grammatical inference: introduction and survey, parts 1 and 2. *IEEE Transactions on Systems, Man and Cybernetics SMC-5* (1975), 95–111 and 409–423.

[22] Gale, W. A., Church, K. W., and Yarowsky, D. A method for disambiguating word senses in a large corpus. *Computers and the Humanities* (1992).

[23] Gazdar, G., Klein, E., Pullum, G., and Ivan, S. *Generalized Phrase Structure Grammar.* Blackwell, Oxford, 1985.

[24] Grefenstette, G. *Finding semantic similarity in raw text: the Deese antonyms.* In *Working Notes, Fall Symposium Series.* AAAI, 1992, 61–68.

[25] Grefenstette, G. Evaluation techniques for automatic semantic extraction: comparing syntactic and window-based approaches. Technical Report, Department of Computer Science, University of Pittsburgh, 1993.

[26] Grefenstette, G. SEXTANT: extracting semantics from raw text: implementation details. *Heuristics: The Journal of Knowledge Engineering* (1993).

[27] Guda, R. V., and Lenat, D. B. Cyc: a mid-term report. *AI Magazine 11* 3 (1990), 32–59.

[28] Hindle, D., and Rooth, M. *Structural ambiguity and lexical relations.* In *Proceedings of the Association for Computational Linguistics.* ACL, 1991, 229 – 236.

[29] Jackendoff, R. $\overline{X}$ *Syntax: A Study of Phrase Structure.* MIT Press, Cambridge, MA, 1977.

[30] Jelinek, F. Self-organized language modeling for speech recognition. IBM T.J. Watson Research Center, Continuous Speech Recognition Group, Yorktown Heights, NY, 1985.

[31] Jelinek, F. *Markov source modeling of text generation.* In *The Impact of Processing Techniques on Communications,* J. K. Skwirzinski, Ed. Nijhoff, Dordrecht, 1985.

[32] Levinson, S. E., Rabiner, L. R., and Sondhi, M. M. An introduction to the application of the theory of probabilistic functions of a Markov process to automatic speech recognition. *The Bell System Technical Journal 62* 4 (1983), 1035–1074.

[33] McDougall, W. A. *The Heavens and the Earth: A Political History of the Space Age.* Basic Books, New York, 1985.

[34] Miller, G., Beckwith, R., Fellbaum, C., Gross, D., and Miller, K. J. WordNet: an on-line lexical database. *International Journal of Lexicography 3* 4 (1990), 235–245.

[35] Pereira, F., and Schabes, Y. *Inside-outside reestimation from partially bracketed corpora.* In *27th Annual Meeting of the Association for Computational Linguistics.* ACL, 1992, 128–135.

[36] Pereira, F., and Tishby, N. *Distributional similarity, phase transitions and hierarchical clustering.* In *Working Notes, Fall Symposium Series.* AAAI, 1992, 108–112.

[37] Resnik, P. *WordNet and distributional analysis: a class-based approach to lexical discovery.* In *Workshop Notes, Statistically-Based NLP Techniques.* AAAI, 1992, 54–64.

[38] Rose, K., Gurewitz, E., and Fox, G. Statistical mechanics and phase transitions in clustering. *Physical Review Letters 65* (1990), 945–948.

[39] Schütze, H. *Word sense disambiguation with sublexical representations.* In *Workshop Notes, Statistically-Based NLP Techniques.* AAAI, 1992, 109–113.

[40] Schütze, H. *Context space.* In *Working Notes, Fall Symposium Series.* AAAI, 1992, 113–120.

[41] Tanimoto, T. T. An elementary mathematical theory of classification. IBM Technical Report, 1958.

[42] Viterbi, A. J. Error bounds for convolutional codes and an asymptotically optimal decoding algorithm. *IEEE Transactions on Information Theory 13* (1967), 260–269.

[43] Winograd, T. *Language as a Cognitive Process, Volume I: Syntax.* Addison-Wesley, Reading, MA, 1983.

[44] Yarowsky, D. *Word-sense disambiguation using statistical models of Roget's categories trained on large corpora.* In *Proceedings of COLING-92.* 1992.

Glossary

$\arg\max_x f(x)$ The value of x that maximizes $f(x)$.   **48**

$\alpha_j(k, l)$ The "outside" probability of a PCFG   **90**

$\alpha_i(t)$ The "forward" probability of $w_{1,t}$ and $S_t = s^i$ **57**

$\beta_i(t)$ The "backward" probability of $w_{t,n}$ given $S_t = s^i$ **58**

$\beta(e)$ The "inside" probability of the edge e **93**

$\beta_j(k, l)$ The "inside" probability of a PCFG   **89**

$\mathcal{C}(x)$ Vector of properties of x (intuitively x's "context")   **136**

$C(x)$ The count of the occurrence of x in some (understood) sample   **39**

$\mathcal{E}^j_{k,l}$ Set of the edges that create the non-terminal $N^j_{k,l}$ **14**

$\bar{\mathcal{E}}^j_{k,l}$ Set of edges that require the non-terminal $N^j_{k,l}$ **14**

$H(n)$ The head constituent of the non-terminal n **131**

$H(X \mid Y)$ The conditional entropy of random variables X, Y **145**

$H(W)$ The entropy of the message W **29**

$H(L)$ Entropy (per word) of a language L **31**

$H(L, P_M)$ The per-word cross entropy of the language L according to P_M **34**

$H(W, P_M)$ The cross entropy of W according to the model P_M **33**

$I(X; Y)$ The average mutual information of random variables X, Y **138**

$I(x; y)$ The mutual information of the outcomes x and y **136**

$M(n)$ The parent (mother) of the constituent n **132**

$N^j_{k,l}$ A non-terminal N^j that dominates $w_{k,l}$ **76**

ω The number of terminal symbols in some HMM   **43**

$\bar{p}$ A non-terminal symbol that dominates a string including a p **8**

$P(N^i \rightarrow \zeta^j)$ The probability of the PCFG rule $N^i \rightarrow \zeta^j$ **77**

$P(s^i \xrightarrow{w^k} s^j)$ The probability of the HMM transition   **45**

$R(n, t_j)$ Syntactic relation between n and $M(n)$ in t_j **132**

$r_{a,b}$ Syntactic relation between head of ath rule and bth rhs constituent   **132**

$S(x)$ The semantic tag of the lexical item x **125**

$\hat{s}^i$ The most probable sequence of states starting from s^1 **56**

$s^i \xrightarrow{w^k} s^j$ An HMM transition from s^i to s^j emitting w^k **43**

σ The number of states in some HMM   **43**

$\sigma(t)$ The most probable sequence of t HMM states for a given output   **53**

$\sigma_i(t)$ The most probable sequence of t states leading to s^i **56**

$V(W)$ The set of values assumed by the random variable W **29**

$W_{1,n}$ A sequence of n random variables, $W_1 \ldots W_n$ **24**

$w_{1,n}$ A sequence of n words, $w_1 \ldots w_n$ **24**

$|X = x|$ The number of times the outcome of X is x **21**

x_i The ith in a sequence of x's—e.g., w_i **24**

$\lceil x \rceil$ The smallest integer $\geq x$ **30**

x^i The ith in the canonical ordering of x's — e.g., w^i **43**

ζ^j Some (the jth) sequence of terminals and non-terminals   **75**

Index

accepting states, of Markov processes, 32
acceptors, *32*
adj, 3
adjective-noun attachment, 20
adjective-noun modification, 129
adv, 3
aligning corpora, 148
ambiguity, in tagging, 49
ambiguous grammars, 6
antonyms, 144
artificial intelligence, 1
attachment decisions, 119
AutoClass, 155
average mutual information, *138*, 46
aux, 3

backward probability, *58*
  algorithm for, 60
  relation to PCFGs, 89
Basili, R., 124
Baum-Welch algorithm, *60*
Bayes' law, *22*
bigrams, 40
binary Tanimoto measure, 142
bits, *27*
Boggess, L., 50
bracketed corpora, 108–111, 117
bracketing, 109
breadth-first numbering, *131*
Briscoe, T., 111
Brown, P., 136, 143, 148
Brown corpus, 48
  number of word-types in, 120
  size of, 36
  tagged version, 49
Buckshot, 155

Canadian parliament, 148
Carroll, G., 105
centroid, *141*, 159
CFGs, 4
Charniak, E., 51, 105
chart, *9*
chart parsing, 9–16, 20, 75
  algorithm, 10, 19
  most likely parse in, 101
  for PCFGs, 91
Chomsky-normal form, *8*
  in grammar induction, 108, 111
  for PCFG proofs, 89, 94
Church, K. W., 50, 52
clustering, 135–136
CNF, 89
code trees, 28, 30
coding theory, 27

computational linguistics, 1
compositional semantics, *17*
compress, 29
co-reference, 19
cognitive psychology, 81
conditional entropy, 138, *145*
conditional probability, *22*
conj, 3
context
  as direct object, 139
  as next word, 136
  in speech recognition, 1
  as syntactically related material, 142
  as word window, 139
context-free grammars, 4–9
context-free languages, 75
context-free parsers, 9
corpus, *24*
cosine, as a distance metric, 154
cross entropy, *33*
  of a language, 34
  as a model evaluator, 34–38
cross validation, *36*
critical points, 104
  in HMM training, 65
  in PCFG training, 98
cycles in grammars, 16

database classification, 1
dependency grammars, *106*, 117
DeRose, S. J., 50
det, 3
distance metrics, 135
dominance, 76
domains of discourse, 125

ϵ-transitions, *43*
edges
  adding and removing, 12
  of a chart, 10
  in chart parsing, 92
  of an HMM, 43
ergodic, *34*, 36
entropy, 27–31, *29*
  conditional, 145
  of a language, 31
  per word, 30
Euclidean distance, *135*
  in sense disambiguation, 154
  in word clustering, 136, 146

features, *3*
file compression, 29
final state, of a finite automata, 32
finite-state automaton, 32